Stop
In The Name Of The Law

By Alex O'Kash

A Savage Press Publication

Additional Copies Available. Use order form at back of book.

First Edition
Second Printing * 500 * April 1995
ISBN 1-886028-00-1

$9.95

Printed in the USA by

M◯RRIS
PUBLISHING

3212 E. Hwy 30
Kearney, NE 68847
800-650-7888

This book is based on my personal experiences, and to a certain extent, events experienced by brother officers who have entrusted me with the responsibility of relating them accurately. With this in mind, I have taken precautions to preserve the anonymity of certain sources. Due to the fact that some of the people mentioned in this book, and/or their relatives, are still living in Superior, I have changed some names and certain other identifying facts to protect the innocent . . . and the guilty.

Acknowledgments:

Stop In The Name Of The Law is lovingly dedicated to my wife, Annabelle, for her patience and support of my efforts in this past year of writing and throughout my life.

Appreciation to my daughter, Judith James, for her editing, typing and many suggestions; To my publisher, Mike, for his encouragement and advice; To my brother members of the department, Ace, Bill, Al and Chet, who helped refresh my memory of past incidents, and Tom, for providing necessary technical information.

PART ONE

SUPERIOR'S GOLDEN ERA

There is an era of time in Superior's history that I felt should be recorded for posterity. It seems that perhaps I am alone in this sentiment, if one is to judge from the lack of any written history of Superior's early days - days when the town was a thriving port of call.

Yet, whenever I begin to tell tales of the years when Superior was referred to as *Little Chicago,* because of its bustling activity and promise of industrial growth, I am met with wide eyed stares and pleas for more.

I am not a historian and the stories included in this book are in no way intended to be an encompassing recount of Superior's history. They are my stories, memories of my youth and the youth of a town that has grown old just as I have.

Perhaps they will inspire someone more knowledgeable than I to record Superior's history in detail. If not, at least there will be this, a few stories from an old man who remembers.

Alex O'Kash

Highbridge Boulevard

It wasn't so long ago, when no matter where you traveled in the States, you were hesitant to say you were from Superior because the usual reply with a sly grin was, "Oh! Third Street."

The city has since changed the name to Highbridge Boulevard, I suppose to erase the stigma and to cleanse the negative reputation resultant of the activities that took place during the heyday of Third Street.

In the winter of 1924 my family moved from a Minnesota farm into the city of Superior. I was three and a half years old. The most memorable event of that exodus was the bitter cold. Riding along the dirt road, the canvas top of our Overland car flapped in the wind. Only the leather straps that anchored the canvas to the body kept the gale from blowing the covering away. I remember sitting in the rear of the large, black touring car alongside my mother, who held my baby sister in her arms. My five older brothers and sisters were cramped in around us. Mother had bundled us in sweaters, scarves and heavy wool coats. Even wrapped in a thick, wool blanket we couldn't stop shivering.

Gazing out the window, I saw only the mountains of snow that bordered the narrow roadway. Snowflakes swiveled in the air around the car and seeped through its crevices, invading our refuge. All I wanted then was to arrive at our final destination and to be warm again.

At last our trip came to an end in front of an old, two story, wood frame building with two large windows and a sign suspended from a cross-pole above the door. I couldn't read but I was sure the sign spelled out SALOON. Neon tubing, in a cool shade of blue, glowed from behind a plate glass window larger than any I had ever seen before. This was the tavern my parents had bought. For the next eighteen years I would live above THE BLUE MOON.

I grew up to the realities of the world at Seventeen North Third Street. I worked in The Blue Moon, swamping floors and cleaning toilets as soon as I could hold a mop. When I was older, I tended bar late into the night. It was in these later years that I truly came to know and understand the goings on of Third Street.

The neighborhood around Third Street consisted of a diverse group of families, mainly Slavic, but also including Austrian, Polish, Lithuanian, Italian and Jewish immigrants. As different as their nationalities, so were their means of making a living.

During the daylight hours Third Street was a typical community, with merchants plying their wares. Taverns, restaurants, hotels, meat markets, grocery stores and rooming houses were in abundance. Housewives hung their wash and prepared the day's meals. Children played in back yards and empty lots when not attending school. Neighbors were closely knit. As a group, they celebrated their respective holidays, marriages, and baptisms and comforted one another through illness and death.

As dusk settled, Third Street changed its colors like a chameleon. Daytime events gave way to the very different milieu of the night. Mothers shooed their children into the house with orders not to venture out. A check was made to make certain that young daughters were safely in their homes. A glance out

Stop in the Name of the Law

the window to the police call box at the corner assured that the night-beat cop was on duty.

Bright lights of hanging beer signs, neon tubing glowing behind dingy windows, and cafe and hotel lights spilling into the street, illuminated the night world. While others in the city slept, Third Street was just awakening.

Gone now is the name Third Street. Gone are all the *houses*, the girls and their pimps, the hustlers, the street walkers and the window tappers. Gone are the clubs, the entertainers and the excitement of a night on Third Street.

Standing at the northern end of Tower Avenue today, looking down Highbridge Boulevard, it's hard to imagine the street was once the site of a thriving neighborhood, much less the hub of Superior's glittering night life.

Let's go back in time. Let's visit the notorious *Red Light District* of Superior's past.

Nigger Brown and Narcotics

In 1931 I was eleven years old. Back then we Serbs were called Hunkies. Polish immigrants were Pollocks and Negroes or African Americans were often referred to as Niggers.

The more polite citizens called him Barber Brown, but he was generally known as Nigger Brown and it was just as generally known that he supplied narcotics to the *tenderloin* district.

His barber shop was on Third Street and Tower Avenue, kitty-corner to the Blue Moon. Late in the evening, cars would pull up and park at the rear of the shop. People would enter and shortly thereafter exit. He did more night business than day business, and he wasn't cutting hair at night.

Brown, black as a moonless night, always wore a ladies silk stocking on his head. He would greet everyone with a smile and a cheery "Hello." My parents sent me to Brown's for my haircuts. Sitting in the barber chair one afternoon, facing the shop's front window, I watched a large, blue sedan pull up in front. Four men in black suits got out of the car and walked toward the front door.

Brown pocketed his scissors and hurried into the rear of the shop. When he returned, he slipped a packet of white powder under the cushion of the chair I was seated on, and instructed me to, "Sit still and be quiet." He casually proceeded with my haircut.

The men entered the shop and the leader, showing a badge, produced a warrant to search the shop. Thus began a lengthy search of the Brown's Barber Shop. Cabinets, drawers, closets and furniture were all thoroughly searched. Suspecting I was sitting on what they were more than likely looking for, I became very nervous, fearing that if they found the hidden bag I would be implicated as an accomplice to the crime - whatever it was.

Probably it was my imagination, but whatever I was sitting on began to feel uncomfortable and hot. The longer I sat and fidgeted, the hotter my seat got. Barber Brown kept clipping away. "Be still," he whispered. "Stop wiggling."

Finally the search ended. Unable to find what they sought, the officers left, saying, "We'll be back again, Brown." As the car drove out of sight, I jumped out of the chair, reached into my pocket and handed Brown the quarter my parents had given me to pay for my haircut

Brown retrieved his bag of white powder, pushed my hand away and said, "No charge this time." With a flash of his pearly white teeth he added, "I have to give you credit, son. You sure were one cool customer."

"Yeah," I thought, "but not as cool as you think."

The Night Life

Cadillacs, Buicks and Packards cruised the streets. Pimps, hustlers, and street hookers started their rounds. The girls in the *houses* prepared for the night's business. The Tenderloin District came alive, welcoming regulars who would spend their money on fleeting pleasures, and enticing innocents with illusions of romantic adventure.

On the south side of Third Street, at the corner of Tower, stood my father's tavern, The Blue Moon. Next came Billie's Bar, then Tony's. Across third street was Club Superior, Kresch's, Eli's, and the Ritz night club. West of Tower Avenue was the Club Chateau, The Main, The International, and Pomithers. South from the corner was the Carlson Hotel, where a fellow, or sometimes a lady of diminished circumstances, could rent a room.

There was no shortage of drinking establishments or clubs for dancing and socializing, but the main attraction wasn't the access to taverns or dinner clubs, it was the access to women. If you asked any sailor, miner or lumberjack what brought them to Third Street, their answer was always, "The girls!".

Across the street from the Carlson was the Douglas

Tavern. Tony, a heavy set man of Italian descent ran the Douglas. Tony was a quiet person who mixed little with his neighbors. His aloof nature generated rumors of his connection with the mob. While Tony tended bar, Rose ran the whorehouse in the rooms upstairs.

Madam Rose met all the customers at the door. She checked every man out to make sure he wasn't the law, and then escorted him to the parlor and took his dollar. Scantily clad women entered the room and waited for the man to make his choice. Each girl hoped she would be the one selected so she could earn her fifty cent cut.

The Douglas was only one of many houses of ill repute. The most commonly known were the St. Paul Rooms, Louise and Stanley's, Indian Sadie's and 314 John.

There were the smaller houses too. They had no names and for the most part were indistinguishable in any way other than the beckoning women in their windows. Walking down the street, a man might hear a tapping on the window. Turning toward the sound he would see a smiling woman who gestured to him to enter her house, but ahead lay another brothel and another possibility. On Third Street a man could *window-shop* an entire twelve blocks and always return to the lady of his choice.

There were *daytime girls*, who were in the windows before noon to catch the early trade, *afternooners*, and of course, *the ladies of the evening*. This feature of the street kept action along the strip lively. Sailors from the ships, miners from the range, and lumberjacks from the sticks contributed to the steady stream of patrons parading Third Street, looking for action.

Whenever complaints of these activities were filed, police would make a raid of the known houses. Oddly enough, male clients weren't present during these raids. The girls, instead of being scantily clad, were fully dressed and ready for their trip to the station. Arrest reports were made on all the women, criminal violations filed and bail set. In the morning the pimps would arrive with bail money. The girls never showed up for their hearings, bail was forfeited and the houses were back to business as usual.

A Young Man's Education

Over the years, working for my father and picking up extra cash running errands and sometimes driving for the local pimps I became acquainted with most of the *gents* of the Tenderloin District. I listened to the tales of their Madams and girls, of the joints they were a part of, and to the details of their private lives.

I was impressed by their big cars, hundred dollar suits and gold and diamond jewelry. There were times, as a boy, when I thought they had the life, and maybe I could have it too. But my parent's values won out, and though I didn't know it when I was in the midst of that seedy lifestyle, I would eventually end up on the opposite side -- a policeman.

Sam, Miltie, Cadillac Hank, Joe D., Joe R., and Ossie were the big operators, the *first liners*. They were sharp dressers, personable, and had charm and the gift of gab. There were other pimps around, nameless small fry who had a girl or two on the line, but it was the pros who owned the Madame's and ran the houses.

These fellows may have been pimps by trade, but in public, in the light of day, they behaved like well bred gentleman.

Stop in the Name of the Law

Seldom did a word of disrespect or obscene remark pass their lips, but compliments were profuse. Every waitress on Third Street was happy to serve any of the *gents*. A guaranteed twenty-five cent tip was a lot of money when her daily wages were only a dollar.

Abe Soroka's barber shop was a frequent gathering spot for the pimps. Abe kept them looking fine and they could hear all the news of the street while getting their shave and haircut. At the Saratoga bar they picked up the daily race tabloid for off-track betting. In Grimsrud's Pharmacy, they played Pan-Ginnie with Miltie and a few old boys. Pan was just a friendly game with a small exchange of money - an afternoon's entertainment.

Sometime in the early afternoon, the pimps would come into The Blue Moon. I listened, from behind the bar, while they discussed girls that were giving them problems and the difficulty in recruiting new girls. I overheard details of their intimate relationships and their casual encounters. It was an education for a boy of tender years.

When talk was over the boys moved on to their nightly stud poker game at Mike Stall's. That is, after they made a short *visit* to their girls, for "love and money," as they called it.

The card game at Mike's was different than the friendly afternoon game at Roy's. This was for high stakes -- no limits. Joe provided the beer, hard liquor and sandwiches. As the game progressed, Joe raked a chip from each pot, and usually on the final bet, took two chips.

When the game ended, the boys walked across the street to Sam Lurye's night club. The Ritz Nightclub always featured a top dance band and the club was filled with the local girls who loved to dance the jitterbug. The Ritz was where I first met Ozzie, and was privileged with a demonstration of the 'Southern Shuffle'.

Ozzie, with his slow drawl, fascinated women from eighteen to eighty. Other men tried to emulate his style, but were mere shadows in his presence. There was only one Ozzie.

He was over six feet tall, wide shouldered, with brown eyes and a perpetual smile. He wore tailor made suits that fit like a glove, and shoes polished to a gleam. Ozzie's speech was smooth. He would say, "You hold them tight, you sway, and then you shuffle." It was just a slight movement to the right and then the left, expending little effort but giving extraordinary pleasure in return.

After dancing at the clubs, a typical night ended around 3 a.m. with a steak cooked to perfection at Milwaukee Joe's. Not long after, the bar lights were tuned off, the doors of the 'houses' were closed and a cover of respectability camouflaged the scandalous activities of Third Street.

The Madams and The Girls

Pat, Rosie, Rye, MayBelle, Edna, Sally and Indian Sadie were the Madams of Third Street's red light district. They ran the brothels with an iron fist, taking pride in running a smooth operation for their pimps.

Each house had at least a half-dozen or so girls. The standard price for a girl was a dollar with a fifty-fifty split for the house and the girl. Once in the room, however, behind closed doors, it was rare if the girl didn't try to make an extra buck. Some of the girls split the extra with the house. Others foolishly tried to conceal it from their Madame. All of the Madams had once been girls in the house -- they knew all the tricks. If they caught a girl trying to hold back there was *hell to pay*. These old gals were tough, and a wallop from them was often worse than what the pimps would give. Eventually, every girl would learn the *house rules* and gladly split any extra money she made.

At least once a month, the Madams wanted out. They were ready to socialize, drink, dance, converse with people, and go shopping to spend their hard earned lucre. On these excursions, they were generally escorted by their pimps. The Blue Moon Bar was the only place on the strip that had a lunch counter. The electric coffee maker perked all day and there was fresh bakery to go along with Ma's delicious sandwiches and soup. The jukebox had all the latest hits from blues to swing, adding one more enticement to make the Blue Moon an enjoyable place for the girls to spend a few hours of leisure.

Soon after they would arrive, a twenty dollar bill would grace the bar and the Madame would announce, "Drinks for the house." When the twenty was used up, it was followed by another, and then another. It was understood that this patronage was *remuneration for referral*, a form of compensation for sending customers down the street with the reminder to say, "I was sent by the Blue Moon."

Shortly before it was time to leave, Edna, one of the Madams who frequented the Blue Moon, would ask me, "Al, can you get us a driver?" This meant they were ready to make the rounds of the other bars and clubs in town and possibly out into the county. The pimps couldn't take the chance of driving while intoxicated and with a Madame under the influence. I'd check with the local lads to see if anyone was available, and when I wasn't successful in recruiting, I chauffeured the entourage myself. The job paid well, depending on the generosity of the Madame, and although it was a profitable source of income, it was one I had to give up at the request of my fiancee.

I also got to know most of the working girls on the line. They, too, had their regular day of leisure. Weekly, they scheduled doctors appointments to check for venereal disease. When they were all done at the doctors office, the rest of the day was theirs.

Some of the times they would come into the Blue Moon alone, other times in pairs and occasionally in a group. The girls were dressed like fashion models, wearing their best attire. Their coiffures were perfection. They were immaculate in appearance, but not in the sense of the conception.

Expensive perfumes surrounded their presence and a radiance of joy emanated from a combination of their drinking and the pleasure of each other's company. It was ladies enjoying the escape of the drudgery of their profession. For the day it was fun and gaiety, tomorrow it would be "back on your back," as they said.

Listening to their conversation, my youthful, vague images of *the life* took on the sharper edges of reality. I came to know that their daily activity wasn't all pleasant. Diane, another regular customer, best expressed the true feelings of it all. "The sooner it's over the better. Especially the part about pretending it was great," she often said.

This pretending, I learned, was the most important part of their job. If a girl wanted a paying customer to return, thus continue paying, she had to make him believe he was better than the average John. "A happy customer is a customer forever," Diane explained.

Dottie frequently complained of men who asked her "What's a nice girl like you doing in a business like this?" Dottie had a stock reply, though, that usually shut them up. She would ask, "Why is a nice guy like you doing business in a place like this?"

I remember one particular exchange between the girls. Ollie, newer to the trade, complained that some of the customers were a little too regular for her taste, even when they only showed up once a month. "Those lumberjacks stink," she wailed. "They wear the same clothes for months on end. They smell like skunks."

Big Alice, an alcoholic, was at least six feet tall and weighed in at more than two hundred pounds. She laughed at newcomers like Ollie. "I don't care where they're from, what they do or what they want. If they got the money, I got the time," she said, plunking down two bits for another beer. "It all spends the same, honey."

Ollie was slender, dark and petite. She wasn't too attractive and I always thought maybe that accounted for her quiet nature. "I have to do this to support my kid," she said. "As soon as I can get a decent job I'm going to quit."

"You'd better find a man too, honey. No matter how you complain now, you'd miss it if you didn't have a man," Alice warned her.

Ollie continued in the business until her young daughter was approaching the age when she would realize how Ollie earned her money. Rather than have her daughter know the truth, Ollie left town, claiming she was through with the business. She was never heard from after that.

Recruitment and Replacement

Often at the bar I listened to the gents discuss their problems with replacement of the ladies leaving the business and recruitment of new gals.

Transportation of a female across state borders for illicit purposes was a federal offense punishable by imprisonment. Therefore great care was taken by the pimps in moving whores from one area to another to avoid detection by law enforcement agencies.

Recruitment of prostitutes for Superior was generally from Minnesota, Illinois and Missouri. It was arranged for the women to travel by bus or train, unescorted. when possible, the women made their own travel arrangements to Superior to avoid any possible connection to a pimp.

Local recruitment was also attempted and at times proved successful. Lottie, who worked the St. Paul Rooms and Lee, from Cadillac Hanks House, were examples of local recruitment.

New girls arriving in the area created a great deal of excitement among regular patrons of the bordelo's. Word would spread like wild-fire, and there was a rush of activity at the establishment of the new arrival. Those who partook of the new girl's services were eagerly questioned by others about her attributes or specialties.

Was she good? Was she white or black? Blond, brunette, or a redhead? did she have a nice shape? Was she young or old? And most importantly, was she worth a buck?

After a time, the excitement receded and the boys wondered when the next new gal would come to town.

The Street Hookers

The girls on the street, working the main drag, were independents. Lone operators, they had no pimps and didn't work in the houses. They did their business in hotels, their apartments, or in the back seat of a car. Most were single -- either never married, or widowed or divorced, but some of the street hookers were married.

Trench Coat Edie, as she was known, was one of the married ones. She made nightly rounds of the bars, sitting at the end, positioning herself so that only her back was visible to the rest of the patrons. When a gentleman would sit beside her, she'd engage him in conversation for a short time, and then let her trench coat slip over her knee and fall open to reveal her naked body. Well, not exactly naked -- Edie always wore a black garter belt and stockings. If the man, in an attempt to seem polite, made any effort to continue the conversation, Edie uncrossed her legs, displaying her goods and naming her price. There was generally very little conversation after that, other than acceptance of her offer. Arm in arm, Edie and her gent would walk to her car where she bestowed wares and collected her fee.

Rita the Red Head had a different approach. She operated a rooming house on fourth and Banks, one block north of Third Street. Her tenants were old retirees, referrals from welfare, drunks and bums. When they got their checks, Rita made sure they paid the rent, and then spent the rest of the month screwing them out of what was left.. Once in a while, between paydays, she would let them charge a piece. Generous Rita usually ended up with every penny they had.

When Rita needed the roof repaired, the furnace fixed or any other job that required a hired man, she would retain men that would take their breaks in bed, and reduce their hourly rate accordingly. Some finished their jobs with little compensation, but with maximum satisfaction.

Out on the street, the men Rita picked up were taken back to the rooming house for their *jollies*. Rita was one of the street walkers known to take on the weirdoes. When they revealed their desires, Rita never flinched. "You name it, I'll game it," she replied, adding, "but honey, it'll cost ya some money." Rita fancied herself a poet.

Ol Tom

The Blue Moon opened its doors at 8 am. each morning, Monday through Saturday, and closed at 1 am. Without fail, as the door was unlocked, there stood Ol Tom. Tom was an elderly Slovenian bachelor in his late 70's. Each morning Tom would be there waiting at the door. He would amble up to the bar, put down his quarter and say, "I have bottle of Northern Beer."

The bar ran a daily special on Northern for twenty-five cents. He would sit and slowly sip on the bottle because this bottle was the only luxury Tom allowed himself daily. Tom was another scrooge, you knew this because he wore the same baggy trousers until the seat wore out, the same shirt until the elbows popped out, and the same coat until the rotted thread parted at the seams. His attire was spotted with the remnants of his previous meals. Tom didn't wash clothing, nor did he have them washed by others. He was never cleanly shaven, always wore a stubble of grayish beard. It was evident he seldom washed. His shoes were scuffed and he wore an old crumpled felt hat.

One morning, Tom walked in with a totally different appearance. Shocked, unable to believe what I was witnessing, I managed the words, "Tom, you look so different. Is there something special going on today?"

In his Slovenian accent he replied, "I have my beer today and a brandy too then I go see the girls."

"See the girls? Tom, you're 78 years old and you're going to see the girls? You can't love those girls no more, you're too old. You're wasting your money."

Angrily, Tom replied, "You tink I crazy, you tink I throw my money away. The girls like me because I still a good man. I know what to do. Rosie tell me I better than her other fellows. You bet she know, she no lie."

I smiled at Tom and served him his beer and bump.

"No, I no waste my money. Tom no dummy," he said to me.

As he departed I recalled the remark Diane made at the bar a few nights previous. "If you can make them happy, they always return, and it's another *Buck in the Bank*."

Homosexuality

Erma and Shelby were the *Mystery Gals*, who worked the clubs. It was a known fact by the boys in town that these two were Lesbians. They sat alone, unescorted, and scrutinized their prey as the unwary victims entered the club. Night progressed and a familiar scenario unfolded.

Erma and Shelby would leave with a man and return about half an hour later. Nobody I knew was ever sure of what transpired --at least, would never admit to knowing, as such knowledge would have to be from firsthand experience -- but there were some pretty wild guesses bandied about. Whatever took place, their was always a divi of the take between Erma and Shelby.

Erma and Shelby weren't the only homosexuals that frequented Third Street. In those days, though, the labels were not so polite. The men of that persuasion were called gays, queers, fruits and fags, but no matter what one called them, on Third Street, there was little objection to their presence or lifestyle.

They came to Third Street for the night life, to drink, dance and sometimes to be *Mary*. They were circumspect, not displaying their affections in public, but neither trying to conceal their preference. Not attempting to conceal their identity seemed to earn them an element of respect on the street. There was less regard for the *closet queens,* professionals and business people in the community.

Among those who thought they'd succeeded at concealing their true nature, were a judge, a scoutmaster, an educator and a man of the cloth. While most of the townspeople had no idea that these men engaged in homosexual activity, it was well known by many on Third Street.

The scoutmaster planned hiking and overnight camping excursions for the young boys of the city. The cleric preached Godly sermons at morning services and dressed in women's clothing at night. The judge visited a Northern Wisconsin resort every weekend, accompanied by his wife and niece. They were welcomed by a handsome young man who worked there and played the role of the niece's beau. The wife, aware of her husband's liaison with the young man,, engaged in an affair with the resort owner. As for the niece, she spent her afternoons sunbathing and walking the beach with her supposed beau.. Little was ever known about her night time activities at the resort, except that they didn't involve that handsome young man.

No account of this element of Third Street would be complete without W.P. He was the Liberace of the lower end and will long be remembered for his music on the keyboard, and the enjoyment by all who listened as he played renditions of the old favorites. He granted all requests, seeming to know every song.

W.P. died in a mysterious and tragic way. Early one winter morning, he was found outside his residence, partially clothed and frozen to death. There was no evidence of any criminal act, but neither could anyone offer any plausible explanation as to the circumstances of his death.

Honey

Stories of the raids on the houses of prostitution along Third Street were common, but one stands out in my mind forever. My appreciation to Bill, one of the officers who participated in the raid, and later related this tale to me.

Arriving for duty, the four PM shift detectives were called into the Chief's office. It seems it was time for a raid to demonstrate to the good citizens of Superior that the local police weren't turning their backs on the moral corruption in the Third Street district.

"Tonight I want a raid on 314 John," the chief ordered. "Arrest Rye, the owner, and all the whores that are working there.

The officers drove two squad units, parking them on Fourth Street, around the corner from 314 John. They discussed their plan of action. Art was selected as the decoy to gain entry into the brothel. Art was a tall blond Scandinavian, former Superior basketball star and professional football player. He appeared the most unlikely of the group to be suspected as a cop.

Taking cover of darkness, he approached 314. Art ascended the steps and knocked on the door. Rye glanced through the peek hole in the door, and, satisfied with her inspection of the patron, opened the door and said, "Honey, you all come on in and have yourself a good time."

Smiling, Art flashed his badge and in a stern voice said, "Police, this is a raid."

Rushing up onto the porch, the other officers forced their way into the premises, displayed the search warrant, declared Rye's a house of lewdness and arrested the bawdy occupants.

The success of the raid was primarily due to Art's performance and his characterization of an innocent customer. From that day forward Art's buddies called him Honey.

Social Security

Though the lewd ladies, and the bawdy houses flourished below the tracks, the ministers, church goers, and the more prudish citizens of the city objected to these activities. So it became necessary at times to make a raid, arrest the Madams and their girls and close the brothels.

The chief of police summoned the detective unit and ordered a raid of the St. Paul Rooms. At midnight, the police entered the yard at the rear of the building and knocked on the door. Nobody expected police at the back door. It was opened without hesitation.

"Sam, this is a raid. We are placing the girls under arrest."

There was rarely any resistance to these raids, and this time was no different. The officers proceeded upstairs and notified the girls to get dressed for a night in jail

Standing at the booking counter, the Lieutenant on duty made out an arrest sheet for each of the girls.

"Next. Name?" he asked.

"Pat." Pat was a very attractive woman, probably the best looking hooker on the street. She was always neatly dressed, slim and curvaceous, and smiled all the time. She was the most talked of prostitute in Superior at that time, and the only one who had to take days off because of being in such demand.

"Age?"

"I'm twenty-two."

The Lieutenant looked up at the woman he was questioning. "For Christ's sake Pat, you've been twenty-two for the past ten years of arrests. When the hell are you going to have a birthday?"

"How nice of you to ask. My birthday is tomorrow, I'll be twenty-three."

"It's a shame you'll never reach sixty-five at this rate. You'll never be eligible for Social Security," the Lieutenant dead-panned.

"Honey, it's a fact, men are lustful. As long as the men are around, I've got all the Social Security I need."

Superior Call Girls

There were maybe others, some who were more discreet, not as public with their avarice recreations. The following are the stories of known married women, who for one reason or another indulged in inappropriate amorous affairs, working as call girls in Superior.

Over the years as a bartender and later as an officer of the law, I came to know who these women were, and the why of their life styles. Some came from the affluent neighborhoods of the city, were housewives and mothers. One was a socially prominent woman. Two were married to men who worked night shifts, allowing their wives the opportunity to engage in these extra marital affairs and pad their pocketbooks. Others claimed they were unhappy, sexually, with their husbands and this was a means of fulfilling their desires. Only one had an arrest record which consisted of misdemeanors; traffic violations and drunkenness, but no arrests for prohibited sexual practices.

Surprisingly, one of the husbands was aware of his wife's promiscuity. I often wondered how many of the other husbands knew of their partners immorality, but exhibited a pretense of ignorance.

A proprietor of a certain North End bar had the phone numbers of three of these call girls. Another of the girls was on call to a cab driver who had fares asking for girls. A night duty clerk at a downtown motel called *Rae* whenever a customer made known his desires for a female companion for a good time.

There is the possibility that some of these gals are still around, so for that reason I have chosen fictitious names to protect their identity.

~

Rusty

We begin the tales of the Superior call girls with *Rusty*, mother of two, married to a truck driver. Rusty only accepted gentlemen *callers* when her husband was on the road.

Rusty was one of the girls available on call from the lower-end bar frequented by sailors. Her reason for engaging in this extramarital activity was that her husband only worked part-time, and she had to earn money to help pay the rent. She told her husband the money came from selling cosmetics door to door.

~

Shari

Shari was a respected lady with two college educated children who had left Superior, relocating to other areas. Her hobby was buying and selling antiques and collectibles. During the day, while her husband worked, she would accept calls from the bar for engagements. Sources stated she had confided to a intimate friend, "If I have to peddle my ass to get money so I can go South in the Winter to see my friends, so be it."

Shari had a real way with words, and used the skill to her advantage. You see, she never really lied to her husband about her extra income. Whenever he asked her where her money came from she simply said that she had , "Sold what was old."

~

Dottie from Duluth

On weekends, while her husband was home, *Dottie* was a faithful wife, performing her homemaking duties. On weekdays, she would accept callers arranged by her lady friend who operated a North End bar. Dottie would shuttle back and forth from the bar to a motel with her Johns.

Dottie explained her life style to her friend, saying she had a strong, constant inclination to perform sex but her husband wasn't cooperative. Her rationale was that what she did was acceptable, as it fulfilled her desires and also filled her purse. She explained to her husband that her income came from tending bar at her friend's tavern.

~

Lady La Du

Lady La Du, young, blond, blue-eyed and shapely, worked as a waitress at a downtown club. Her husband frequently made out of town, overnight stays in connection with his job. No matter how often she had sex with her husband, it evidently was not enough, as she was consistently involved with more. The cabby who drove her to work and again drove her home, supplied her with his fares seeking sex. The cab driver was happy because he got an extra tip. La Du was happy and temporarily satisfied, and in addition, she got revenue. She didn't have to explain added income to her husband; most of it was lost in the bar at Sylvia's dice table.

~

Rae

Rae was on welfare, with a husband who was a drunkard and contributed little to the family's income. Rae's friend next door was the night clerk at a downtown motel. He knew of Rae's difficulties and need for money.

Single men checking in at the motel would inquire where a fellow could go into town to have a good time. The clerk would mention some clubs that had good bands and attracted large crowds. He would then call Rae and give her the room number of the check-in. Only blocks away, Rae would hurry to the motel and sit in the lobby. Wearing a short skirt, she would cross her legs and smile at the guy when he entered the lobby. Usually this behavior proved successful. She notified the gent she was available for sex at a price. At this point the pair would generally retire to the gent's room. Once again, Rae was pleased to be able to make a little extra cash, the gentleman was pleased with the entertainment and the clerk at the hotel was pleased with his cut. In this case, even Rae's husband was pleased. The more money Rae had, the more he stole from her purse for booze. Now the other bar owners were pleased too because Rae's husband was a good paying customer.

Call girls contributed to the good of the community in many different ways.

Nightmare at the P.D.

Saturday night was always a busy night for the Police Department in Superior. The taverns closed at 1 a.m. Clubs in town operated until three. Among the nightclubs, were Burgraff's, Club Superior, Tony's, Mary and Nicks, Main Nite Club, Emil and Jeannie's, Club International, Pomither's and Sam Lurye's Ritz.

Most of the clubs had music on Saturday night. Club Superior had entertainment also. Two shows nightly, with either Clark Brown, or Lou Streeter as M.C. Shows were brought in from the cities, and included singers, dancers, magicians and strippers. Tony's always had the best dance music in town, especially when Frankie Cox was playing his horn.

Goebels Beer was ten cents a bottle and went up to fifteen cents during the floor show. The entertainment drew large crowds from nearby towns as well as Superior.

At 3 a.m., the clubs closed but the partying continued. Liquor was still available by the bottle at Rydell's Drug on Sixth Street and Tower Avenue. A knock on the back door and an exchange of money provided one with a fifth of booze if it was intended for medical purposes.

The Bartenders Club, on Seventh and Tower opened it's doors at 3:30 am., exclusively for bartenders and their friends.

However, tavern owners and their friends were also admitted. In those days, everyone was a tavern owners friend.

You could also journey to Oliver, Wisconsin, just a short drive south of Superiors town limits. Oliver bars were open all night and always had bands for dancing.

If you preferred, you could remain in town, buy a six-pack or a bottle, go to Milwaukee Joe's restaurant or the Saratoga Cafe, buy a cup of coffee and sit and guzzle all night.

For party goers looking for a good time it was *Hello Superior!* Prostitution, gambling and twenty-four hour gin mills - who could ask for more?

PART TWO

THE OTHER SIDE OF THE STREET

Placing my left hand on the Bible, raising my right hand, I repeated the oath given to new officers, "I Alex O'Kash, having been appointed as a member of the Superior Police Department in the City of Superior, Douglas County, Wisconsin, but have not yet entered upon the duties thereof, swear that I will support the Constitution of the United States, and the Constitution of the State of Wisconsin, and will faithfully discharge the duties of said office to the best of my ability, so help me God."

I Was then handed a Smith and Wesson .38 caliber revolver, a thick leather belt and holster, hand cuffs, flashlight and night stick. My badge number was 39. Sergeant L. Jacobson told me to report for duty at 8 p.m. that night.

That was in December of 1955. I was 34 years old, had a wife and three children. For the next twelve years I wore badge number 39 and fulfilled the duties of a law officer to the best of my ability.

The following stories are true experiences which occurred during my tenure as a police officer for the city of Superior. Some of the names, places and incidental characters have been changed to protect the innocent -- and the not so innocent.

THE ROOKIE

Assignment One

The first two-week shift on the job I walked the Sixth and Ninth Street beat. All patrol officers assembled in the squad room, checked the log book and dispersed on our respective assignments.

Sgt. Francis, took me in tow. Walking from the station on Broadway and Hammond we proceeded to Tower Avenue. Heading north on Tower, we came abreast of Byrne's Bar. The Sergeant and I entered the bar and stood by a counter at the entrance. We were soon greeted by Tommy, the owner of the establishment.

I was introduced to Tommy as the new officer on the force. Francis explained I would be working this area for the next two weeks. Tommy turned and picked up a package of Lucky Strikes, and placed them on the counter in front of Francis. He then asked, "The usual?" and returned with a dark colored beverage in a heavy bottomed, *high ball* glass. Sergeant Francis partook of his refreshment and we left Byrne's. At the next Bar, Zannie's, the identical routine was repeated.

Back outside on the beat, Sergeant Francis explained to me, just what my job entailed. "When bars and stores close for the night, you check the doors and windows for break-ins, and you check again before quitting time. If you find a broken window or an open door, call the station and make a report."

I listened to my instructions with the serious intent expected of a rookie officer.

"I'll see you again about midnight, and around 3 a.m.," he told me before walking down the street and turning the corner.

Sergeant Francis must have encountered some problem after he turned that corner, because I didn't see him for the rest of the night.

~

Assignment Two

The next two weeks I worked the day shift and was assigned to the motorcycle patrol as a traffic officer issuing parking tickets. Riding down the street, I put chalk marks on the tires of parked vehicles. Allowing two hours of free parking, I returned after the grace period to check for violators. The offenders were ticketed and fined one dollar.

The next day, I was stopped frequently during my routine patrol by people with tickets who explained the extenuating circumstances for the overtime parking. At that time, an officer was allowed to excuse the ticket if he deemed the reason was worthy. Of course, everybody thought they had a worthy excuse - "I just had to run in to pay my electric bill so they wouldn't turn my lights off.", "I had to call home. I forgot to turn the oven off.", "I had to go to bathroom."

This privilege was soon discontinued due to abuse. Eventually the city installed parking meters and the motorcycle patrol became a thing of the past.

My biggest problem with this particular assignment wasn't the pleading housewives or the belligerent businessmen. Until my first day on the patrol, I had never driven a motor cycle.

Explaining this to the commanding officer I was told, "Go down to the bay-front and practice. When you have the hang of the bike, come back."

Fortunately for me, it was a three wheeler with a side buggy, although even those features didn't prevent me from tipping. During those two weeks, I sustained bruised ankles and skinned elbow and knees. Accustomed to a brake pedal on the floorboard of a car, it took a major adjustment to adapt to the brakes on the handlebars.

Though I was happy with the termination of this assignment, the neighborhood kids weren't nearly as pleased. In fact, they were downright disappointed. Each afternoon while I was at home for lunch, the kids took turns sitting on the bike, making "har-rumm, har-rumm" noises. After I'd eaten, each child, seated behind me with their arms wrapped tightly around my waist, was allowed a brief ride before I departed.

Their laughter and squeals of delight gave me great satisfaction, but the biggest thrill was hearing each little boy say "When I grow up, I'm going to be a policeman and ride a motorcycle."

~

Assignment Three

During the third two weeks of duty rotation as a rookie cop, I was assigned to patrol in a squad car on the eight o'clock shift. The squad man I worked with was Morgan. Morgan was a veteran officer of twenty years. A tall, wide-shouldered man of Scandinavian heritage, he was easy going and got along well with everyone. All the men on the department respected Morgan.

I doubt there was ever a more dedicated officer on the Superior force. It was an extreme pleasure to work with him and after the two weeks, I told Morgan I wished we could be assigned as permanent partners. Morgan already had a partner but said that maybe someday in the future it might be possible.

As it turned out, I did get a chance to work with Morgan for over a year. This was very beneficial to me because not only was he a dedicated and hard working police officer, he excelled as a teacher. He was firm but diplomatic, well liked by the public, and adept at handling all calls and emergencies, attributes, I aspired to.

I remember one call Morgan and I answered together. It was a report of domestic abuse. From the address dispatched to us, we knew immediately the husband in question was a repeat offender. It was relayed to us that his wife reported he was armed and would *take care* of any policemen that might respond to her call.

Arriving at the residence, looking through the front window, we could see the husband sitting on the davenport facing the front window with the rifle propped up alongside the arm rest.

Morgan said to give him five minutes to enter the home from back and move in behind the husband. When I saw Morgan moving into the room, I stood clear of the front door and shouted, "Police! Open the door!"

I expected the front door to be blasted, but there was no sound other than Morgan calling for me to come into the house at about the same time the wife swung the door open.

Morgan held the rifle. A check revealed that it had not been loaded. The husband was drunk as a skunk, bluffing as he had done many times in the past. One of the things I learned from Morgan was to never underestimate a situation, no matter the past history of the perpetrator.

Had officer Morgan desired, I'm certain he could have attained higher rank in the department, however, he seemed content with his status. Perhaps he knew something all along that I only found out after years on the force.

Following street and squad duty, my assignments for three years, I was finally assigned to work at the desk as a dispatcher and booking officer, plus handling juvenile problems in the absence of Honey. I was bestowed the chairmanship of the Annual Policemen's Ball, and the Superior Police Department Children's Christmas Party. I was also elected as a representative for the police union. All of the above for a monthly salary of $450.00, which was paid bi-weely at $225.00.

This was when a man working on the docks, loading grain or cargo was making $11.00 per hour. Skilled craftsmen earned approximately $9.00 per hour and a sandwich with a cup of coffee cost $1.00.

From my princely sum of $450.00 came deductions for Federal, State and Social Security withholding; life and medical insurance premiums, and other miscellaneous deductions such as union dues, leaving me with very little to take home.

The low pay was a negative factor of police work, but the positive side for a family man was having job security and a pension.

I guess I have to admit though, that what kept me working on the Superior Police Force for twelve years was the satisfaction derived from knowing that I was helping people and serving my community, the same motivation in Morgan that I'd admired as a rookie.

THE NAKED TRUTH
A Trilogy of Bare Facts

~

The Chase

"Squad seventy-seven, check on a report of a public disturbance in the seventeen hundred block, Maryland," the radio blared.

Responding with a 10-04, I proceeded with the siren howling and the roof light flashing. I arrived at the scene to observe a completely nude young women standing at the rear of a residence screaming and sobbing. As I approached she saw me and began to run. Not knowing what her problem was, I followed her in pursuit. She ran through the neighborhood, between houses, and around a garage and into a field. Doors began opening and people emerged to investigate the commotion. Dogs, excited by the running humans, were alerted, and shortly were at my heels barking and yapping. The kids in the area chased after the dogs, and motorists stopped to observe the show. The field was wet from recent rains and the quarry, attempting to elude me, splashed through one puddle after another assuming I would give up the chase.

"Stop in the name of the law," I ordered, but my command went unheeded.

In order not to be outdistanced, I followed my prey through every puddle, splashing mud and water on the dogs, the kids, and mostly on myself.

Finally, with a last ditch flying tackle, I managed to stop her. There I laid, in the mud atop a naked, writhing woman. The dogs sniffed and circled, the kids laughed and the drivers left their cars to get a closer look at the entertainment.

I'd called for assistance before giving chase, so a squad car and back-up arrived within seconds. They immediately covered the woman with a blanket and put her into the squad car. The woman, obviously suffering an emotional breakdown, was taken to the local hospital for attention.

The next day I was reluctant to return to work, knowing the jokes I would be subject to from my fellow officers. There were plenty, but the one I will always remember was the homemade plaque that read,. "Rain, snow or sleet, to Officer O'Kash for his notable *feet.*"

~

H. Lush - Shay

She came from a rural farm area north of Ashland. A country girl that liked the big towns and the entertainment and excitement they provided. Hazel had a problem. She was an alcoholic. Friendly when sober, she was mean as a skunk when drunk. Superior, *The City of 100 Taverns*, was a favorite boozing place that fulfilled Hazel's needs and desires.

Hazel was youthful, blonde, attractive and shapely. Always dressed to perfection, she made a dazzling entrance into any room. Her smile attracted all the gents and she hustled them for drinks with suggestive conversation that led them to believe possibilities of a promising rendezvous existed. More often than not, Hazel's only rendezvous on any given night was a date with the local police.

Generally, as Hazel drank more her personality and behavior changed dramatically. When, eventually, she was refused more drinks because of her inebriated condition, Hazel became combative and threatening. Vulgarity, insults and curses that could make a sailor blush spewed from her mouth punctuated by a glass thrown at the bartender.

One night was a little different than all the rest. The police were summoned. Hazel was placed under arrest, and transported to police headquarters. She was confined in the first women's cell block at the end of the corridor where she would be visible for routine checks.

Shortly after her booking and lock-up, a peculiar gurgling was heard. Checking on the noise, I found Hazel trying to commit suicide by hanging herself. She had fashioned a noose from her belt tied, together with other articles of clothing, and suspended it from the top cell bar. I immediately cut her down. I took the belt, the blanket from her cot, and any other items I thought she could use to fashion a noose, from her cell.

When I checked on Hazel later, to see if she was all right, I found her standing at the cell door completely naked.

"Let me out or I'll stand here all night if I have to," she screamed. She refused to cover her body and she was in full view of anyone coming into the station.

All the men in the station came into the hall to witness the commotion. Someone suggested we get the police camera and take a picture "to be used as evidence".

When the officer returned with the camera he stepped in front of the cell to focus for the shot. Hazel turned around, bent over and *mooned* the camera, shouting, "Focus and kiss this, and I hope you choke."

Still refusing to dress, Hazel was left to her ranting and the men returned to work.

Early morning came and an entirely different person exited from the cell to appear in court. Too embarrassed to look at anyone, she only gazed at the floor, remaining silent except for her soft spoken plea of, "Guilty," in answer to the judge's charges.

~

Eino The Exposer

The Wisconsin Block was located on Fifth Street, between Hughitt and Hammond Avenues in Superior. The Wisconsin Block apartment building housed mostly senior citizens, almost all elderly widows, and Eino Rivila and his brother Tiovo.

Eino, in his early 60's was a laborer on the Soo Line Railroad. These men were commonly referred to as section hands and gandy dancers. They repaired and replaced faulty railroad tracks. The work required carrying railroad ties and 120 pound sections of steel track, besides tamping the rock bedding for the track and driving the spikes. It required strong men who could work an eight hour day. All of this heavy labor made Eino a muscular, very powerful man.

Officer Bennie Lugouwski and I were on routine patrol in squad 75 when we received a call to check on a disturbance at the Wisconsin Block.

"Damn," Bennie exclaimed. "I just lit this cigar."

There was nothing Bennie enjoyed more than puffing on a good stogie. After spending a shift in a patrol car with him I smelled like a stale cigar. My wife said she always knew when I was working with Bennie the minute I walked through the door upon returning home. With one hand on her hip and the other stretched out to receive my clothing, she'd wait while I stripped down and then send me off to the shower, putting my clothes directly into the wash.

Bennie doused his cigar and I knew from his grumbling that he was in an ugly mood because of it. Bennie weighed over 200 pounds, was athletic and as strong as an ox. I tipped the scales at 180, had spent years as an amateur boxer in my youth, and occasionally lifted weights to stay in shape. I guess you could say Bennie and I were a force to be reckoned with, and with one half of the team already disgruntled, things could get even uglier than Bennie's mood.

Climbing to the second floor of the Wisconsin Block, Bennie and I encountered several elderly women gathered in the hallway. Dressed in their bathrobes and slippers, with curlers in their hair, we wondered what could have induced them to be seen in such a state.

As we neared, we were even more dismayed to see Eino, standing in the middle of the throng, completely naked. The women were yelling at him, he was yelling back, and Bennie was yelling at all of them.

"What the hell is going on here?" my partner demanded to know.

A chorus of agitated, female voices answered all at once.

"Eino always walks from the bathrooms to his room naked. We asked him to stop and he just won't," one of the women complained.

"We want him arrested for indecent exposure," another insisted.

I asked Eino why he persisted in this activity.

"Every Saturday I take da Finnish sauna in da shower. Den I walk to da porch to rub snow on my body like we do in da ol country."

"But, Eino," I reasoned, "your nakedness embarrasses the women. They don't want to see you this way."

"I no ask dem wimin to look. If dey don't like, dey no have to watch."

"Eino," Bennie said from behind clenched teeth., "you could wrap a towel around yourself to cover your peter for Christ's sake."

I asked the ladies for a blanket and was quickly handed one. Reaching over and taking a hold of Eino's arm, I tried to wrap the blanket around him. Bennie had taken Eino's other arm.

"No!" Eino hollered. He pushed Ben against the wall and sent me rolling down the hallway like a bowling ball.

I quickly recovered my balance and rushed back to assist Bennie who was making another attempt to subdue Eino. My lunging tackle was ineffectual against the stalwart Finn. It was then that the ladies decided to help and several of them jumped into the fray.

We finally managed to wrestle Eino to the floor, but in the process, several of the ladies robes had been torn open or tugged off, leaving them as exposed as Eino.

Bennie and I subdued Eino and held him while the women regained their composure and their bathrobes.

We were reluctant to arrest Eino, but had no choice as the women were even more insistent, having suffered such humiliation in front of Eino.

Bennie, in no mood for anymore nonsense, hustled Eino off to his room and made him get dressed before we took him to the station.

The landlord was pressured to evict Eino and the old ladies were happy at last. At least most of them were. I learned much later, through the North End grapevine that one of the women had confided to a friend after the incident, that during the commotion someone had grabbed her by the crotch.

"I don't know if it was Eino, one of the other women, or one of those nice policemen, and I don't care," she reportedly said. "It felt so good I had an orgasm - the first one since my husband died."

I wondered many times after that if Eino's brother Toivo honored the Finnish Sauna tradition and also strolled naked through the halls of The Wisconsin Block. If he did, the women weren't complaining about it anymore.

Indian Sadie's
and the
Hard-Headed Swedes

Bernie O'Connel was the owner and operator of the Black Cat Cafe. The officers on the Superior force always went there because Bernie was so generous. Evidently, someone convinced Bernie to join the police force, which he did.

One afternoon my partner, officer Hilden, and I got a call to Indian Sadie's whorehouse to assist an officer. When we arrived, there were three men involved in a fist fight on the narrow walkway that ran between Indian Sadie's and the building next door. Officer O'Connel had been called to the scene and was having little success in breaking up the fight.

Bernie said they were Swedish sailors off a foreign ship that was in port. He had attempted to break up the fight with little success. A huge heavyweight sailor was beating his shipmate while the third man was trying to stop the fight. They evidently understood little or no English as they did not respond to Bernie's command to "break it up."

I tried a simpler order. "No. No. No more fighting." It also failed to stop them. In fact, the aggressor started to push and shove us while we attempted to subdue him and the other combatants. As a final effort, the pugnacious perpetrator was sapped on the head with a gauged blow from my night stick. I expected him to be slightly dazed, but to my surprise he merely turned to me and said, "No more do that, I take away and hit you."

Well, at least we knew then that he understood English, and while we tried to reason with him, the other two men ran.

When he discovered that the objects of his attack were gone, he turned and walked up the stairs into Indian Sadie's

We decided not to pursue the matter any further. We had fulfilled our commitment to assist an officer.

Better to leave the problem to the ship's captain, who probably had more experience dealing with hard-headed Swedes.

Domestic Dispute

"Al, Check on a complaint of family problem at the Wisconsin Block."

As I entered the building, I heard loud voices that seemed to be two people arguing. I knocked at the door of the apartment and was greeted by a woman with bruised and swollen lips and a bloody nose.

"Is there a problem here, Ma'am?"

"This is the problem." She gestured to her battered face. "I didn't get this from bumping into a door. "That S.O.B. did this to me." She pointed to a man sitting across the room. "And it isn't the first time!"

"Okay. Try to calm down now."

"Get that bastard out of here. I never want to see him again," she shouted at me.

The man in question remained unruffled. I turned toward him and asked, "Did you do this?"

"Officer, it wasn't my fault. I just stopped to have a couple for beers after work. When I walked through the door she threw a pot of beans at me, then she picked up a pan of wieners and started swinging at my head. I *deflected* the pan and it hit her in the face."

The wife was quick to refute his claim. "Liar. You liar. I'm getting tired of you're boozing and carousing around with other women. I know who you're shacking up with."

"Officer," her husband pleaded with me for understanding, "I've never cheated on her - I swear it."

"You lie as much as you cheat," she accused him. Turning to me she repeated, "Get that bastard out of here?"

"Lady, are you telling me to arrest your husband."

"Do whatever you have to. I want him out!"

"Are you willing to file a complaint?"

"You damn right I will," she answered my question.

"Okay buddy, looks like you're going to have to come with me." I took him by the arm and led him downstairs and out to the police car. I opened the door of the squad and ordered him to get it.

Throwing both arms up to the roof of the vehicle to brace himself, he refused to enter.

I reached for my handcuffs and attempted to cuff the prisoner, but he was quite strong and wasn't cooperating. I dragged him down to the sidewalk, straddled his back and tried to cuff his hands behind him.

Suddenly, something struck me from behind. Turning, I saw his wife, her eyes blazing with fury. She began assaulting my head and back with closed fists.

"I said take him in, not beat him."

"Lady, that's what I'm doing - trying to take him in." I was trying to ward off her blows with one hand, while still holding onto the prisoner with the other.

"Let him go. You're hurting him," she screamed at me.

I released my hold on her husband, standing up to face the agitated woman.

"I never told you to beat him up," she said, running to his side.

"Lady, the hell with you and your husband. Fight your own battles."

Alex O'Kash

Getting into my squad, I glanced back to see them arm in arm, smiling and walking up the stairs. Radioing the dispatcher I reported, "Domestic dispute settled with utmost diplomacy. Complainant pleased with official resolution of problem. Returning to patrol duty."

Traffic Cop

The public's concept of law enforcement generally flows along the lines of murder, rape, robbery and assault. True, these crimes do occur even in a small town, but the majority of police work in Superior involved routine patrol duties.

A good deal of the police work I did was related to traffic violations and motorist accidents. One particular case which I have often enjoyed relating involved two motorists in a collision at the intersection of Broadway and Hammond Avenue, a busy downtown intersection.

The driver of vehicle one, an elderly motorist drove through a stop sign and collided with vehicle two, driven by a mature female, hitting it broadside.

Investigating the accident, we notified the driver of car one that we would likely be charging her with an arterial violation.

"Well officer, it wasn't my fault," she protested. "It was her fault."

"But lady," I reasoned. "You drove through a stop sign."

"Well if she had been paying attention to what I was doing and where I was going I wouldn't have hit her. She caused the accident when she drove in front of me. Why don't you charge her with inattentive driving?"

We advised her that at her court appearance, she could plead not guilty and tell her story to the judge. In parting, I suggested that it might help her case if she secured the services of a good attorney.

The driver of the second car expressed concern that she might have to defend her innocence and perhaps should hire an attorney as well.

I assured her it wouldn't be necessary, the judge would rule fairly.

Looking back, I recall the reactions that story usually elicited, the general consensus being that it was absurd for the woman of the first car to think she could blame the second driver. Now, it seems to be a common occurrence, and I don't doubt that today, with two experienced attorneys going to bat, the driver of the second vehicle would no doubt be assigned some percentage of fault.

The Skunk Caper

"Squad 72 , check on a complaint of a skunk on the premises of 52nd and Tower."

Arriving on the scene, there stood a group of people on the corner watching a skunk digging for insects in the front lawn of the residence.

"Officer, I want you to get that skunk out of my yard."

"Ma'am, this is a little out of our line of work" I said. "I suggest you call the D.N.R."

"I already did, and they said to leave the animal alone and eventually he would return to where he came from."

"I'm afraid I'm in complete agreement with that suggestion."

"Yes, but it's smelling up the whole neighborhood, and it's ruining my lawn," she lamented.

"We can report it to the pound master - see if he has any solutions. Maybe he can set a trap."

"As a taxpayer of this city I demand you do something now. If you don't, I'll call the mayor and notify him you refused to take any action in the matter."

Turning to my partner, Jack, I asked, "Have you got any ideas?"

Jack had competed in many state pistol shooting competitions. He was rated an expert marksman and had won top awards in team and individual categories. He took out his .38 and said casually, "I'll try to kick up some dirt in his face. Maybe it will scare him away."

Moving the crowd back to clear the area, I gave Jack the OK.

Taking careful aim, he fired and dirt splattered the body of the skunk. The animal raised its head, looked around and turned his body away from the gun fire, raising its tail.

Jack quickly repositioned himself and took his shooting stance. He aimed carefully and fired again.

Dirt spewed up in the face of the little creature. Looking around in bewilderment, it ducked its head low but refused to give any ground.

"Well I guess there's just one way to solve this problem," Jack said. Raising the pistol again, he sighted and fired. At the same moment, the skunk moved and Jack missed by a hair.

Turning, the skunk raised its tail and let fly its protective scent, hitting Jack dead center on the first shot.

Backing away, cursing the animal, Jack leveled his .38 again with the intent of finishing off the little predator.

Before Jack shot, the skunk thumped the ground with her paw several times and three small babies came from underneath a nearby woodpile.

We all watched, a little amazed at the sight of mother and babies skittering off into the grassy field.

Jack lowered his pistol and said, "It's lucky she was a better shot than me, I guess." Turning, he headed for the squad car.

I neared the squad, but the *perfume* emanating from Jack was just too much.

"Jack, I've had to put up with your smelly farts every time we're on patrol together, but I absolutely refuse to drive with you this time."

Calling for a back-up for transportation, I returned to headquarters and reported , "Situation resolved. One officer disabled - unfit for further duty today."

Charlie Bud

Charlie bud was the meanest, toughest orneriest individual that walked the streets of Superior.

Every officer on the beat at one time or another had a tussle with Charlie. When a squad got a call regarding him, a back-up squad was always dispatched. It usually took three and at times as many as four policemen to subdue Charlie.

A call to 75 stated that there was a knife fight at the Club Superior and Charlie Bud was involved. On duty in 77, R.T. Martinson and I were called for back-up.

When we arrived on the scene, the officers had Charlie handcuffed. Sergeant Sharon told me to get in the back of the squad with the prisoner while they went into the club to look for the other participant of the ruckus..

Charlie complained that the cuffs were too tight and asked me to take them off, promising he'd cause no trouble. I unlocked the left cuff to loosen it a little. Charlie swung over and hit me along side my head. I saw stars, flashing lights and heard bells.

Somehow I managed to get Charlie on the floor between the front and back seat and laid on top of him until Sharon returned.

At headquarters Charlie resisted all the way to the cell block. At the cell entrance he grabbed on to both sides of the door and refused to enter. The chief, who was in the station at the time, pushed and shoved Charlie, trying to get him into the cell. Charlie turned around and kicked the chief. It was probably the first time and maybe the last time the chief ever punched anyone.

It didn't make any difference how often he was arrested for drunkenness, fighting or marital abuse, Charlie was combative and resisted on every call.

My worst encounter with Charlie was a wrestling match that ended up with me, my partner and Charlie rolling down a flight of stairs, out the door and onto the walk.

Some of the men on the department were an even match for Charlie. Bob B. and Big Ray, two solid guys, both took Charlie down single handily at different times. Maddie and Peck, in 71 could deal with him effectively. He showed respect for Morgan, and Beech who would tackle him like a hound dog fighting a bear. I was told that Vinny whipped his butt in a street fight. I didn't witness the fight, but would have relished seeing it.

Although it was a dangerous assignment, I rather looked forward to a match with Charlie. I recall often saying to him, "Charlie, we can do this the easy way or the hard way, take your choice." I was quite surprised the one time he said, "Okay, no fight. Let's go."

When I left the department, Charlie was still around. It was a relief to think, *Good-bye Superior P.D. and Good-by Charlie.*

The Creatures

"Squad 77, check on a call from 34th and Hammond. Complaint of an attempted forcible entry."

"Ten-four," my partner Bob replied. Activating the lights and siren he jammed the accelerator to the floor.

"Whoa, Bob. Slow down. There's a full moon tonight," I reminded him. "That's the house the creatures invade."

Arriving at the residence, I knocked on the door. "Police! Open up!" First I heard the lock on the doorknob tumble, then the dead bolt clicked, followed by the slide of another lock and finally the jingle of a chain lock.

Entering, the four security devices were immediately locked behind us again. The resident, an elderly woman turned to us and said, "They're back again. They're coming in on the phone wires, the electric wires and through the keyholes." Drawing the window shades she pleaded, "Do something."

Assuring her that everything possible would be done to get rid of them, we then inquired if she had any relative or friends that she could stay with for the night.

"No one."

"We'll notify the phone company, Ma'am, and the utility company."

"And the Air National Guard to check the area for invaders from space," Bob added.

On a more serious note I told her we'd cruise through the area until our shift was over and then it would be daylight. "Now relax and don't worry. The situation is in good hands and under control."

Leaving the house I looked up in the sky and I would have sworn there was a smile on the face of that 'ol moon.

Triple A's
Alton, Al & Alex

~

Reach Out and Touch Someone

I was fortunate to have worked with the other two *Als* of Superior's police force on a few cases.

Al was a highly intelligent, dependable partner. Alton, A.K.A. Jake, was independent in nature, but extremely capable and dependable in all dangerous situations.

On one occasion Al and I received a call to check on an armed individual at the Saratoga Cafe. Responding to the call, we were met at the front door by the waitress who notified the police department of the situation. She immediately informed us that there was a man on the premises armed with a revolver, holed up in the telephone booth, threatening violence. She elaborated that earlier the man had been seated at the counter and went into the booth to make a call. she said he appeared to have been drinking and upset. Soon after entering the booth, he began yelling and swearing at the party he had called.

The waitress walked over and told him to stop the commotion or get out. He then flashed a pistol and threatened the waitress. Al asked the waitress in what hand the gun was held. She informed us it was in his right hand.

Al formulated a plan of action. He would enter the restaurant through the back door and kitchen and work his way around behind the restaurant booths to the right side of the phone booth. I would maneuver along the south wall to the left of the booth. Positioned, we would wait for some exposure by the gunman. An opportunity was presented when he thrust his head out to survey the surroundings.

Al seized his right hand and wrist and disarmed him while I forced his other arm behind his back. Restrained and taken into custody, the assailant was booked and charged with assault with a deadly weapon.

Returning to the Saratoga for additional information from witnesses, we were rewarded with a free cup of coffee, but I had to pay for my doughnut.

~

The Bank Robber

Called to investigate a report of a suspicious acting individual at Gappa's Tavern, Alton and I were dispatched from headquarters to investigate the complaint.

Met by Gappa, we were informed that the renter upstairs in room number 1 had a shotgun in his possession. Given a description of the individual, we realized it matched the poster of a wanted criminal.

Earlier in the week, a bank robbery had been committed in a near-by Minnesota Community. The robber had used a sawed-off shotgun in the bank heist.

The door to room 1 was wide open and the room appeared unoccupied. Alton entered the room and began to look

Alex O'Kash

around the premises while I waited at the door. Lifting the pillow on the bed exposed the sawed-off shotgun. Checking the weapon revealed it was loaded with two shells. Alton ejected the shells and replaced the weapon under the pillow. Alton then stepped back into the hallway at which time we heard the toilet flush in the small bathroom across the hall from room one.

Motioning me to take position on one side of the bathroom door, Alton covered the other side. As the man emerged from the can, we immediately recognized him to be the wanted bank robber.

Alton drew his .38 and said, "Police. You're under arrest."

The man was taken into custody without any resistance, and escorted to police headquarters. He was booked for suspicion of robbery. Shortly thereafter he was extradited to the State of Minnesota.

The Point

Friday and Saturday nights we always received calls from worried parents.

"It's 12 O'clock and our daughter hasn't returned home from her date; she had strict orders to be home by ten-thirty."

This would prompt us to begin a check of the secret spots of seclusion for teenagers.

Generally the first area checked was Wisconsin Point, with miles of wooded shoreline along Lake Superior's shore. If the parents had reported that their daughter was supposed to be in a group, we looked for bonfires on the beach.

As expected you would find the gang drinking, empty beer cans littering the sand skirting the fire site. Checking names for the missing girl, the kids were told to break up the party and get home. A warning that we would follow up with a check with the parents, usually proved successful.

If the girl wasn't found at one of the fires, the search continued with a check of all the parked cars. A flashlight into the interior of the parked vehicle would often reveal unclothed couples participating in illicit activity. Again, names were asked and if the young lady was the missing person, she was placed in the squad car and returned to her home.

We would inform the parents of her whereabouts and activities, usually describing the action as "necking with her boyfriend."

The boys parents were also notified and told that this practice could have serious consequences. At this point, the father was taken aside and informed of the extent of the "necking." This usually elicited a twinkle in the father's eye, despite his serious frown. I was always sure he was remembering his younger days and visits to The Point.

The old adage was likely true, "Like father, like son."

Stud McKirk

Making a nightly check on Wisconsin Point, my partner and I saw two cars bumper to bumper with no occupants visible in the rear vehicle. Thinking this an odd manner of parking, we stopped to investigate. Flashing a light into the first car we observed a young man and a woman fornicating in the back-seat and an elderly man sitting in the front seat watching the show.

We immediately recognized the young man who ran a car parts junk yard in the city. Puzzled by the couple's conduct, we asked if someone would like to explain.

The lady responded, "My husband is impotent. I still want sex and my husband allows me to if he can watch."

"Is this true?" I asked the husband.

"Yes it is." he nodded, affirming his answer.

"Why on Wisconsin Point? If this arrangement suits you all, why don't you do it at your home?"

"Because I have a twenty-one year old daughter at home and I don't want her to know about this," the woman answered.

The young McKirk, well known by members of the police department, had exited the car by this time, tucking his shirt back into the top of his trousers. Told he could be charged with lewd and lascivious conduct, he promised not to return to the Point again for his illicit sexual activity.

"We'll use the house in future," the husband assured us.

"No," McKirk answered. "We'll get a motel room or use my apartment."

At this point, McKirk took us aside to elaborate. He explained that he had met the daughter earlier when she had come to the junkyard. She was looking for a part for her 65 Ford Mustang convertible. Following a few more visits from her, they became quite friendly and eventually they became sexually involved. McKirk finished his tale by confessing that her parents didn't known about his relationship with their daughter and she certainly didn't know that he was screwing her mother.

My partner and I just shook our heads in amazement.

Once again McKirk apologized for engaging in illicit sexual activity in a public place, and begged us not to pursue this with criminal charges. All I could think while walking back to the sqaud was that revealing McKirk's activities would surely be a case of indecent exposure.

Turkey Johnson

The Johnson brothers were from the lower end of town, below the tracks. The neighborhood was referred to by some as the slums of Superior.

The older of the brothers had a long list of petty arrests and was constantly in trouble with the law. They both frequented the lower end bars, buying when they had the money, bumming when they didn't and at times stealing to provide funds for drinking, or as was the case once, for a good meal.

When the bars closed at 3 a.m. in Superior, the crowds would go to the Saratoga restaurant or Milwaukee Joe's cafe. Johnson preferred Joe's. There, if you concealed your bottle you could continue to drink. If you didn't have a bottle, you could usually find someone who did.

This particular night, Johnson was broke and unable to bum from anyone with a bottle or a six-pack. Disgusted, he headed through the kitchen for the back door exit . As he entered the kitchen, there was nobody present. The oven door was open and there sat a turkey, fully cooked to a crispy brown, cooling before serving. Johnson picked up the pan and disappeared out the back door.

When Joe returned to his kitchen and discovered that his turkey was missing, he reported the theft to the police, with the information that everyone in the restaurant saw Johnson exiting through the kitchen.

Working the lower end beat I was contacted and notified as to the crime. Searching the area, I encountered Johnson. Asked if he knew anything about the turkey, he asked me, "What turkey?"

He insisted he knew nothing about the bird and stuck to his story throughout my questioning. Fed up with the constant problems caused by the elder brother, Chief Buchanan called him into his office the next morning and suggested Johnson had better move to another area or the next time he was brought in, the chief would pursue efforts to have him committed for lengthy confinement as a habitual offender.

The story spread through the lower end that *Turkey Johnson* was being trotted out of town.

Weeks later, standing on the corner of third and Tower, watching the night clientele exit from the Club Superior, I saw Turkey Johnson standing by the door. Walking over, I faced Turkey and reminded him the chief had given him a *floater*.

"You were supposed to get out of town and stay out," I told him.

"I am a citizen of this country and nobody can tell me to get lost, not you and not Buchanan," he answered.

"Then I guess you're coming with me," I informed him.

I took him by the arm and walked him over to the phone on the corner. I had never perfected the technique of holding a prisoner with one hand, searching for a dime to make a call with the other hand, and then trying to dial headquarters for a pick-up squad.

Realizing his opportunity, Johnson started to pull away and I preceded to restrain him. He swung and hit me along side the head. Regaining my balance, I struggled to cuff the prisoner. In the melee he fell, hitting his back on a fire hydrant.

He fell to the sidewalk, moaning, "My back, my back."

I called for the pick-up squad and Johnson was transported to headquarters. As was practice in those days when doctors still made house calls, the doctor was summoned to the station rather than taking the prisoner to the hospital.

The next afternoon I reported for duty. I was summoned to the chief's office and notified that Turkey Johnson was suing me and the City of Superior for police brutality and bodily injury. He had hired a prominent law firm to take his case.

Examining my report of the incident, the chief stated there would be a full investigation, assured me that there was no wrong doing on my part and that I would be vindicated.

When I reported for work the next afternoon, I was summoned to see the chief. He informed me that he had called the attorney representing Turkey to come to headquarters for a conference. The chief stated that, after a lengthy discussion, he had convinced the attorney that he would regret it if he prosecuted me and the city.

The attorney, a long time friend of the Chief, stated that he would make an effort to get Turkey to drop the charges, on the condition that Turkey would be allowed to stay in town as long as he stayed out of trouble in the future.

The following day, the chief informed me that all charges had been dropped. After that, I was careful not to ruffle the Turkey's feathers.

Lucre

Art Buchanan, Superior, Richest Chief of Police in the State of Wisconsin.

This was the headline of an article published in the daily newspaper of a major Southwestern city in Wisconsin, and reprinted in Superior.

Following the publication of the story, many rumors flourished in the community as to how this wealth had been accumulated.

One of the most predominant theories was that the source of Chief Buchanan's great fortune was from the prostitution trade in the downtown, lower end of the City, Third Street.

As a member of the police force at this time, I was questioned by friends and relatives as to whether there would be any type of investigation into the matter.

My impartial response then was that I would be interested to see if the article, combined with the rampant, unsubstantiated rumors would have any effect on the *red light district,* and that perhaps they should reserve their opinions until that time.

To this day, nearly twenty years since I served as a policeman for the city of Superior, I am still asked my opinion in the matter. It would be a glaring oversight for me to neglect this subject, causing those who remember the rumors to stir them up again. I will state unequivocally, that I have no first-hand knowledge as to the accuracy or falsehood of the rumors.

I will say that the news story did trigger some concern by the operators of the houses. Overhearing some discussion by the people in the trade, there was good reason to believe that compensation was part of the game. However, keep in mind that those in the trade may have had reason to sabotage, or undermine the local Chief of Police.

I can only attest to what I observed nightly between 2 and 3 a.m. when I worked the grave-yard shift. A high ranking police officer on the Superior force would make a tour of the area whorehouses. Talk had it that his mission was two fold, infatuation with one of the prostitutes and her services, and the possibility that he was collecting some type of kick-back.

A second interesting scenario that aroused suspicion was a local merchant who was also a city councilman, providing a card room at the rear of his premises. This room, or more accurately, the game, was provided for the afternoon pleasure of the pimps who gathered to play pan-ginnie. The establishment in question was also frequented by the prostitutes to get prescriptions, cosmetics and other personal items.

An older officer on the force offered his opinion that this was an ideal situation for an exchange, stating that the merchant was a personal friend of a close relative to the Chief. As both the prostitutes and the pimps had well known reasons for frequenting the establishment, nobody would be suspicious of their coming and going.

It was also reputed that any message the boys or gals on the strip wanted to convey to the upper echelon of government in Superior could be relayed to the councilman,, who would in turn pass it on to the relative, who again passed it to a third party of high ranking status. That is the sum of the rumors, or proof, as some like to call it, that circulated at the time in question.

It is also a well known fact that anyone in a public office makes one enemy for every friend. There will always be those who condemn - and there are always those who support.

Supporters of Chief Buchanan stated that he was a very conservative, thrifty individual and had made prudent investments over the years which resulted in his wealthy status. A probability no more beyond the realm of possibility than the elaborate rumors that circulated at the time of the article.

The Record

Bennie Davis was his name, a resident of the *East End* neighborhood of Superior. A friendly, likable person, he never gave the police a bad time. Bennie had one aim in his life - to have the *record*. His goal was to attain the highest number of arrests for drunkenness in Superior.

Involved in many of Bennie's arrests, I never did ask him why he had chosen this particular objective. I have often wished that I had inquired, to understand the basis of his endeavor.

Ben would drink until he reached the point of intoxication and then would go out on the street, staggering and stumbling until some citizen would report the problem and a squad would pick him up and take him to the station. While being booked, Bennie would always ask, "Am I still number one? Do I still have the most arrests?"

Assuring Bennie that his record was safe made him happy and back to the cell he would go to sleep it off, smiling all the way.

Reluctant at times to arrest Bennie, because the fine for drunkenness was ten dollars, plus a 7 dollar court cost, many of the officers on the force would offer to take him home instead.

"No," he objected. "I have to maintain my record."

If all the fines that Ben paid were totaled, they may have produced another record for moneys contributed by one individual for arrests.

Bennie always bragged about his record and seemed to take pride in his achievement. I doubt that the Guinness Book of Records listed a category for that type of performance, but then, I never have checked. Who knows, maybe that was Bennie's goal, to get in the Guinness Book of Records.

Cabbies

As a police officer I found it advantageous to maintain good relations with cab drivers. The cabbies would often lend a helping hand to an officer alone on the Third and Fifth Street beats who found himself in a difficult situation. If the cop needed assistance, cabbies radioed their dispatcher and in turn, the dispatcher would call police headquarters.

Tip Top, Saratoga and Yellow Cab were the three main cab companies in Superior, owned by Ben Hoppe, Rex Bowser and Jim Corbett. Drivers were Smithy, Al White, Corbett, Carmine and Bob.

The drivers worked twelve hours a shift and were paid forty percent of their fares. In the 1940's, with approximately 130 freighters sailing the Great Lakes between Eastern cities and the Twin Ports, an average of four to five lakers would arrive daily in Superior. With crew sizes averaging about thirty men, there were over one hundred sailors, many looking for a cab, on any given day in Superior.

Cabbies waited at the dock for their fares. The first request of the passenger was usually to go to the saloons on Third Street. Bob stated the sailors were very generous with tips. The second request, was for the cabby to return in an hour for transportation to a house of ill fame. It was common practice for the cabbies to escort the sailors to the door of the brothel to make certain the operatives knew who brought the customer.

Once a week, a fat money envelope was sent by the Madame to the cab dispatcher's office for the driver. Bob stated that at times he received four to five envelopes a week and smiled all the way to the bank.

Occasionally a seaman would fail to return in time when a ship left port. If he was lucky, Berthiaume's bum boat would get him to the ship before it cleared the harbor. If not, it meant hiring a cab to the Soo Locks in Michigan - a trip of 400 miles, and a nice days wages for the cabby.

A lucrative sideline for the cab drivers was the sale of booze. Most cabbies carried a case of whiskey in the back trunk. At 2 a.m., after the bars closed, sailors wanted to get a bottle. Bob said he would make a pretense of going for liquor and would tell the passenger that because it was after hours he would be charged ten dollars a pint. In a good week, he managed to dispose of a whole case of whiskey.

Cabs were equipped with two way radios between the dispatcher and the drivers. All drivers heard communications between all the cabs and the dispatcher. Bob recalled an amusing incident with a rookie driver on his first day on the street.

One afternoon, when most of the cabs were hauling city residents, Bob had two women passengers returning home from church. The rookie called the dispatcher and said, "I've got a load of sailors who want to go to a whore house. Where are all the whore houses?"

Needless to say, there were many embarrassed drivers and blushing lady passengers. As the dispatcher could hardly answer the question, knowing it would offend paying customers, he sent another cab to intercept and take the rookie's fare. Bob said they spent a couple of hours that afternoon educating the rookie.

Superior was a wide open town for gambling. Bob stated on weekends they picked up gamblers at the Great Northern depot coming in on the afternoon train from Minneapolis, and points south. Bob loaded three to four gents in the cab when there was a shortage of cabs available. The passengers expected to split the fare between all occupants. Bob said they were surprised when he charged each of them full fare.

The assumption existed that driving as a cabby was a low income occupation in Superior. Bob and the other drivers perpetuated that belief to the public to insure the secrecy of their bonanza.

Bobo The Poacher

As I previously stated, a policeman's lot was a poor man's job. Four hundred and fifty dollars a month minus tax withholding, medical and life insurance deductions which all substantially reduced the take-home pay. Additional mortgage and car payments, school tuition and miscellaneous costs of living added to a low income status.

Most officers held part-time jobs or operated some sort of business venture to supplement their income. In my case, I purchased a tri-plex residence, living in one unit and renting the other two units.

Checking the daybook at the police station before going out on patrol, one item stated headquarters had received several complaints of hunting and discharging a firearm on the Archer-Daniel's grain elevator property. Corn spilled along the railroad tracks leading to the elevator attracted pheasants nesting in the area, and made Archer-Daniel's prime hunting grounds.

Cruising down Winter Street, I headed for the bay front to make a routine check of the area. As I neared the waterfront, I observed three men walking in the field, carrying a shotgun.

I drove up to the trio, parked the squad and walked over the hunters. I immediately recognized the men. Bobo Olson, Russ Dalbec, and Cliff Hammer.

"Fellas, are you aware you can be arrested for hunting in the city limits, not to mention that pheasant is out of season?"

Bobo, holding the shotgun, replied, "We weren't hunting."

"Well then, how about discharging a firearm in city limits?"

"We didn't fire the gun."

I reached over, confiscating the weapon. Breaking it open at the breech, I sniffed the barrels. There was no odor of gun powder.

"Maybe you didn't fire it today, but someone was here last week and they left carrying two dead pheasant, the description witnesses gave pretty well fits you Bobo."

"That wasn't me, that was Mick," he informed me.

He didn't offer Mick's last name and I didn't inquire. Even with a name, proving the violation after a week's time had passed would be difficult - certainly the evidence had been consumed by then.

"Well what the hell are you doing here with a shotgun if not hunting?" I asked.

"We were going to throw targets over the water and shoot at them," Bobo replied with innocence.

"Lucky for you that you hadn't fired that shotgun. If you had, I'd arrest you."

"Lucky for you I didn't fire the shotgun," Bobo rebutted. "If I had and you arrested me and you put me in jail, I wouldn't be able to pay you your rent."

Exasperated I answered, "Yes, Bobo, but maybe next time it will be another officer - one who isn't as understanding as me, and while you're in the slammer, welfare will pay your rent."

The Good Neighbor Policy

Located on Fifth and Tower was the Arcade Saloon. Upstairs was the Savoy Rooms, a local whorehouse operated by Madam MayBelle. Across the street, at 502 Tower was Eddie Sax's bordello, run by Pat.

Standing on the corner outside of Herman's Pool Hall at 3 a.m. I heard a commotion at the rear of Sax's building. Checking the noise, I encountered two men who were kicking and pounding the rear door of Sax's establishment. I ordered them to stop the disturbance, then asked their reason for such behavior.

"This is a whorehouse, isn't it?" they asked.

"That's your reason for making such a racket?"

"We've come all the way from Thunder Bay and we want a whore, and this is a whorehouse. We want to get in."

Whatever it is, the door is locked and you're disturbing the peace, so take a hike fellows or you'll be spending the night in a jail cell."

"Just a minute officer," they protested. "This is a public place of business, and we're not leaving until they open the door."

Walking over to the La Fayette Bar on Fifth and Ogden, I called headquarters to dispatch a squad. Returning to the scene I notified the two Canadians that they were under arrest.

I seized one by the arm and the other one panicked and fled. When the squad arrived, we searched the area for the escapee, and in the search process, we found a vehicle with a Canadian license plate. A stake-out of the car succeeded in apprehension of the second violator.

No serious crime had been committed, and the owners of the business establishment hadn't filed any complaint. A truthful answer to their inquiry as to whether or not the establishment was a whorehouse would have been difficult, so as a good neighbor gesture, all charges were suspended. After all, the only real crime committed had been *disturbing the piece.*

Above and Beyond The Call of Duty

On occasion, there were times I would accept official duties that were not a requirement of my job. In the realm of law enforcement, this could be anything from guard duty for hire, to acting as an officer in non-patrol or office situations. These two stories relate such work outside the realm of routine duties.

~

Journey of Love

Louie Ban was candidate for Douglas County Sheriff. As he was a personal friend of mine and a fellow Democrat, I supported him in his campaign, which was successful. Louis was elected to the office of Douglas County Sheriff.

In appreciation, I was issued a Special Deputy Sheriff's card which opened opportunities for me to take on optional duties that would net me extra pay.

Louie was an easy going, likable and friendly person with a knowledgeable law enforcement background. One afternoon he called inquiring if I was available to transport four females patients from the Parkland Health Facility, which housed the developmentally disabled and chronically mentally ill, to the state Facility in Madison. I was to provide my own vehicle and gas the round trip paid $80. I would also be allowed to take a matron along who would be paid fifteen dollars. I asked if my wife could act as matron and was told that would be acceptable. This brought the total extra income to $95.

I discussed the offer with my wife and we decided to accept. The money would pay for a week's vacation at a cabin in Lake Nebagamon.

Thursday at 7 am, I arrived at Parkland to pick up the passengers. I became very concerned when Louie told me no restraints were necessary.

"They won't be any problem, Al," Louie said. I've told them we're sending them to visit with their boyfriends for the weekend. In fact, I expect them to be very cooperative."

Louis' prediction proved true. There were no problems from the onset of the journey. We sat two of the women in the rear with my wife in between, and the other two in the front with me. The trip was rather entertaining, what with the conversation among the women, who were describing their plans for the weekend.

Jane, a pretty girl with long dark hair and a perpetually serene expression on her face, said "I'm not doing a thing this weekend that can't be done in bed with my boyfriend."

Lorraine, who had a more animated countenance than Jane, and the habit of twirling her hair with quick, agitated rotations announced, "When I get my Jim in my room, I'm going to lock the door and throw away the key. Believe me, I know how to make a man happy."

There seemed to be some one-up-man-ship in Alice's reply, "I won't have to lock the door. Once I get my man in my arms and show him my style of lovin', he won't ever *want* to leave."

Marriane, who appeared to be the youngest, and was certainly the most star-struck of the four, declared in a wistful, near whisper, "Ray and I are going to get married. I'll never have to go back to another hospital again."

Our first stop, marking the end of our duties, was the Clark County Hospital, where we dropped off Jane and Lorraine. Then we drove to Winnabago State Hospital and delivered Alice. Finally, we said good-by to Marriane at the Mendota State Hospital, her new home.

Though the trip was somewhat enjoyable, there was a lingering aspect of sadness. There were no boyfriends waiting. There were no romantic weekends in store for these unfortunate women. It was just a shuffle from one institution to another, and a continuation of the existence and treatment (sometimes less than humane in those days) they'd received at other hospitals.

Driving home in near silence, we contemplated our involvement in being party to the ruse perpetrated on these women. My wife and I agreed we would never again go along with falsified information or promises in a similar situation.

~

Another Pill

Once again, Louis came in to headquarters to inquire if I was interested in a transfer of an inmate to the State Hospital in Mendota for evaluation. Making arrangements with Whitney, a fellow officer, to take my shift, I agreed to make the trip.

The following morning at 7 am, I reported to the Douglas County Jail to pick up the inmate. This time my wife was along, not in an official capacity, but as company for me. I signed the necessary papers and took charge of the prisoner. I was then notified that my passenger was a narcotic user and had just been administered a *fix* that would last for approximately four hours. I was given a package of pills and told to dispense them at four-hour intervals. There were no restraints provided and I was told there was nothing to worry about as long as he was sedated.

Two hours into our journey he began asking for his pills, saying that the effects of the previous dose had worn off. I told him he would have to wait another two hours and he became very agitated. Stating that we absolutely had to abide by my instructions, I refused his insistent requests. After a half-hour of his continual begging, we relented and gave him one of the recommended dosage of two pills.

About mid-way to our destination, his behavior began to change radically. He acted irritable, belligerent and overly nervous. He said he was in pain and needed more medication.

Fearful that he would become violent, we gave him the remaining two pills. My wife became frightened that he would try to harm us, so I had her take over the driving while I sat in the rear of the car with the patient.

With over a hundred miles of our excursion remaining, my wife drove at speeds near 80 mph. She was hoping to be intercepted by a State Patrolman and informed me in no uncertain terms that when that occurred, "The State Police can darn well take this nut off our hands." She declared she wouldn't take no for an answer.

As it turned out, we were never stopped by the State Patrol, and my wife drove the remaining miles to the Mendota State Hospital. She was one happy lady when we turned Bill over to the hospital staff.

That was the last time we engaged in escorting patients or prisoners for Louis. We both agreed there had to be an easier way to make a buck.

School Days

Returning home in 1946 after four years of service during World War II, there were limited opportunities for employment. Fortunately, as part of our discharge we were entitled to *52-20*, fifty-two weeks of unemployment insurance at twenty dollars a week. There was also the opportunity to attend college at ninety-two dollars monthly.

Many of my buddies enrolled at Superior State University, so I followed. Four years later I received a Bachelor of Science Degree in Education. My State license was for teaching on a high school level. Graduating in May, I attended a career day seminar at the University. A recruiter from Metropolitan Insurance convinced me to accept work with their agency. I soon realized this was not a vocation to my liking and resigned.

Next, I became involved in selling vacuum cleaners, but soon determined this was not something I desired for a lifetime pursuit.

So it was my sixth place rank on a police examination that finally decided my future. Tied with Bob Bennett, we both became police officers.

Soon after my appointment to the department, I received a call from the Superior School District Board of Education asking me if I would be interested in substitute teaching. The pay was fourteen dollars a day. Working the 4 PM to midnight shift at the police department, I was also able to do substituting to supplement my income.

~

Central High

My first call was to sub for Fran Paquette, teacher and Assistant Dean at Central High School. Fran warned me it was a Senior class in History and they were pretty rough on subs. I accepted.

The day I arrived to teach, I walked into the class in full uniform. The students assumed I was there on police business. I removed my hat, jacket and belt, with all the police apparatus. Then I took my night stick in hand and standing in front of the group I whacked my palm several times before announcing, "My Name is O'Kash, and I'm your substitute."

Later, when principal Brown opened the door to check, he could have heard a pin drop. Looking around, he nodded and smiled before leaving.

The following day, Fran called to inquire how it went.

"No problems at all. Call anytime," I answered.

~

Northwestern

Northwestern was competing in a State Basketball Tournament. I was hired to substitute for the gym teacher, who coached the team. The office informed me I would have several classes of boys phy-ed and also classes of girls phy-ed. I was told, "Be sure the girls shower after gym."

However, no instructions were given as to how to handle this procedure. Used to the routine at the police department, where matrons were called in to handle female prisoners, I expected some female assistant would arrive to supervise the showering. Certainly that had to be the answer.

With fifteen minutes left before the bell, I nervously looked around for assistance, but no help arrived. Blowing the whistle I shouted, "Okay, to the showers, and everybody shower."

One voice from the crowd asked, "How ya gonna know?"

"There will be a check, " I replied. My comment caused quite a stir.

When all the girls had left the gym I went to the main office seeking help. The office clerk stated she had no idea where I could acquire female assistance. "I'm afraid you'll have to handle the situation on your own," she said.

Leaving the office, still puzzling over my dilemma, I reasoned that nobody expected me to actually confirm whether or not each girl had showered. Returning to the gym, I positioned myself by the bleachers and questioned each girl as she came back into the room.

"Did you shower?" I asked. Each girl nodded, answering in the affirmative as she passed by. Simple observation told me that most of them, if not all, were telling me the truth.

I heard the talk in the shower room had been, "Do you really think he'll come in to check? He's a policeman, maybe he can do that."

I guessed that, fearing the possibility of an actual check and the probability that at least some of the girls believed I had the authority, *all* of the girls were compelled to shower - whether it was their normal practice or not.

On the next call to substitute as a phy-ed teacher, I made certain arrangements were made for the supervision of the girls showers.

~

Cathedral

Called to substitute at Cathedral, a Catholic High School in Superior, I reported to the main office. I was informed I would have five periods of instruction and one free hour.

Each hour a new group entered the classroom. The instructions left for me indicated that the subject matter also changed with each class. It was a challenge just to keep track of what I was teaching to which class.

Prepared to leave the room for my free hour, I was surprised to see a group entering. When they were seated I informed them there must be some mistake as I was to have a free period. They seemed as confused as I.

Excusing myself, I went to the principal's office for an explanation.

"Mr. O'Kash, I was just coming to see you," the principal said. "That's Father Meuleman's religion class. Father's been called for an emergency so we had to send the group to you."

"Sister, I'm not qualified to teach religion. I'm not even a Catholic, I'm Orthodox."

Not missing a beat she exclaimed. "Wonderful. You can discuss the schism of 1472 - the Western Church assuming the designation of Catholic and the Easter Church the Orthodox title."

"But I don't know anything about your faith."

"Ah, faith." She glanced heavenward, hands clasped together, pausing for just a moment before returning her attention to me. "You'll do just fine." she said, placing her hand on my shoulder and directing me back toward the classroom.

Returning to the students, I spoke mainly of the Orthodox religion and doctrine, being more knowledgeable of that subject.

Later that afternoon when Father Meulemens returned, he came to inquire how the class went.

When I accepted the substitute position at Cathedral, I thought that, in a strict Catholic School, for once I wouldn't have to call on any of my police training. Father's question, however, compelled me to use some of the psychology I'd learned in relation to negotiating and dealing with the public.

"Excellent, Father," I answered his question. "I believe I succeeded in converting your whole group to the Orthodox faith."

My next call to Cathedral did not include a class in religion.

All In The Family

Being a police officer in a town the size of Superior, sooner or later means that a call will come concerning your own family. In fact, it seems that any unfortunate circumstance always occurs when the officer is away from home, on duty.

Over the years I was called several times. Sometimes my wife would reach me directly at the desk, and at others, dispatch would take the call and relay it to me in the squad. On a few occasions, by an oversight or some breakdown in communication, I was sent on a call not realizing it involved my own family.

Some calls were more worrisome than others, and some were downright frightening.

When my oldest daughter, Linda, was a child, we had a harrowing experience. Sliding down a snowy slope with neighborhood friends, Linda completed one run and lay at the bottom of the hill, laughing, as children will often do. Another sledder had started down behind her, and unable to control the sled, ran over my daughter. The blades of the sled went across her face, slicing into her flesh.

Linda walked home and when my wife opened the door she was confronted by the ghastly sight. Unable to dial the phone, she called out for a neighbor. I received the message to go home immediately, may daughter was badly injured.

Thankfully, Linda's injuries were not as bad as they appeared. She had no visible scars thanks to the outstanding skill of the doctor who stitched the cuts in her face.

When my second son was very young, he had the habit of wandering away from home. My wife would call to say she couldn't find Dan and the patrol cars would start the search. It got to be pretty routine, and thankfully, not cause for much concern.

Of all the family calls I received while on duty, the following three are the most memorable.

~

The Midnight Intruder

"Check on a call of an intruder at Thirteenth and Harrison."

Arriving on the scene, my partner and I recognized the residence as a sorority house used by college students attending the State University in Superior. At the entrance was a barefoot co-ed with a blanket draped over her head and wrapped around her nightgown. Her face was barely visible.

"Dad, it's me."

I was shocked to here my oldest daughter's voice.

"Linda. What are you doing here?"

"Tammy and I are spending the night with one of the girls in the sorority. Mom said it was okay."

Tammy and my daughter had been friends since high school. Now, in their first year at the university, they still did everything together. "Who called the police?"

"I did." Her voice was shaking and high-pitched with fright. "It's here somewhere."

"What's here?" I asked

"I don't know. Tammy and I were sound asleep when I was awakened by a hand or something. It brushed across my face. I screamed and woke Tammy up."

"Where's Tammy now?" I inquired.

"She locked herself in the bathroom. I told her someone was in the bedroom and she started screaming too, then she ran to the bathroom and locked the door."

We entered the house with routine caution, but knowing the active imagination and impressionable minds of young women, I suspected there was no real danger.

Ascending to the second floor, I looked down the hallway to see an array of seemingly disembodied heads poking out of barely opened doorways. As we walked along the hall, Linda close at my heals, she paused by the bathroom door. "You can come out now, Tammy. My Dad's here."

The bathroom door opened and out stepped the frightened young girl, also clad in a nightgown. Visibly trembling, she looked around, her blue eyes wide with fright, and then dashed back to the bedroom.

In a quivering voice, my daughter continued. "They told us the main entrance is left unlocked for other tenants, anyone could get into the building."

I was more convinced than ever that my daughter's imagination had gotten away from her. We always kept our doors locked at home, something my wife insisted on since having a complete stranger enter our home one day when she was alone. I was sure that Linda had been quite uncomfortable knowing the house she was in wasn't secured.

Checking the entire apartment and the outside area, no intruder could be found. I informed the girls that we would patrol the area the rest of the evening, and assured them no harm would befall them.

Returning on patrol, I informed the dispatcher all was clear and we would be on a coffee break at the Blue and White Cafe. Discussing the call over coffee, we wondered if the girls were having delusions or fantasies of a prowler, or if maybe they were the victims of a prank being played by some batty co-eds.

Our coffee was interrupted by a call from the dispatcher informing us that the intruder had returned to the Harrison residence.

Returning to the apartment, we rushed upstairs. Amid screaming and crying, they stated, "He was back again, he was in the bedroom again."

This time, all of the girls in the house were in a state of panic. An immediate search of the area was made and failed to locate the culprit.

"He was patting my face and brushing my hair. It woke me up," Tammy said. "I screamed and he left."

Checking the area again, we were puzzled, as there was no evidence of a prowler. I was beginning to wonder if this was some kind of sorority initiation for my daughter and Tammy. I was about to give them both a good lecture on making false reports when something made me reconsider.

At the end of the hallway was a door leading to the attic. As there was a chain lock in place, we hadn't checked it previously. I took my weapon in one hand and flashlight in the other. My Partner slowly opened the door and I directed the beam of light into the darkened interior.

With a swish like a gust of wind and the fluttering of dozens of wings, a hoard of bats flew out the door, over my head and over the co-eds huddling behind me.

The screaming girls fled down the stairs and out the door, with the bats in pursuit. At least the panicked girls thought the creatures were pursuing them. In truth, I think the frightened animals were simply looking for a means of escape.

A further check of the attic revealed it was infested with bats. Wide gaps in the attic floor and the ceiling and baseboard trim of the girl's bedroom indicated that the bats were the real intruders.

Calling the station we reported that the problem at Harrison had been resolved, the intruder had been identified and our initial assumption had been right - something about the whole situation was batty.

"Squad 77 returning to duty."

~

Hide and Seek

"Squad 77, check out a family problem on Sixteenth and Hammond. The caller said they'll be outside waiting."

Hearing the address jangled my nerves a little. I lived on Sixteenth and Hammond. Arriving on the scene, I was at first relieved and then once again concerned when I saw a large group of people, most of whom I recognized, gathered in my next door neighbor's backyard.

My wife broke away from the crowd. "Alex," she said, her voice breaking. "Judy is stuck in the chimney."

My eyes shot up to the roof of our three story house.

"Not the house. In Cleary's barbecue chimney."

Our neighbor's had recently built a patio barbecue out of cement blocks. Working my way through the crowd I saw my seven-year-old daughter's head poking out of the top of the chimney.

My two sons, Tim and Dan were rolling on the ground with laughter. My eldest daughter, Linda and her cousin Sheryl were trying, without much success to stem their laughter. All of them were suffering my wife's anger, who didn't find the situation amusing in the least.

"Judy, what are you doing in that chimney?" I asked.

"I was playing hide and seek with the rest of the kids and I climbed in here. My head was sticking out so I bent down so nobody would see me."

Her brothers howled with laughter.

Judy's eyes began to tear. I can't get out. My knees are stuck in something."

My wife swatted at our sons, Tim and Dan, in a futile attempt to stop their laughter. "Get out of here. This isn't funny."

"Her knees are probably stuck in the hole for the flu," my neighbor explained. We tried to get her out, but we're afraid we might break her legs if we pull to hard."

Alex O'Kash

The enormity of the situation and the reason for my wife's concern became clear. I tried to calm my daughter, assuring her that we knew how to get her out. Then I instructed my partner, in a whisper, to radio headquarters and tell them to request assistance from the fire department.

Unfortunately, my sons heard me.

"What's the matter, Dad? You afraid she's going to go up in smoke?"

The Eighteenth Street Fire Station was only blocks from our home. Within less than a minute of my partner's call, we heard the engine's siren wail.

The firemen assessed the situation, then began chipping at the mortar below the lowest block of the chimney. When all the mortar had been loosened, they lifted the block carefully away from the body of the barbecue, releasing my daughters knees from the eight inch hole.

They laid the section of chimney on the ground, Judy wiggled from her confinement, then scrambled to her mother's arms.

After a brief conversation with my wife and a warning to my sons not to further agitate their mother, I returned to duty.

Back on patrol my partner asked me, "Didn't you get called home not long ago to bring the same daughter down from the garage roof."

"Yes, " I answered. "Tim and Dan put her up there so that she couldn't follow them."

"Do you think her brother's may have put her down that chimney for the same reason?"

"Oh, they've gotten much craftier than that. Now if you were to ask me if they devised the game of hide and seek and suggested a few good hiding places, I may have a different answer."

"It's gonna cost a few buck to repair that barbecue," my partner said.

"Yes." I contemplated his observation. "But something tells me that I just acquired a strong negotiating tool for increasing my sons' chores in the near future."

My partner radio to headquarters. "Squad 77 back on duty. Problem resolved to the satisfaction of both the caller *and officers*."

~

Superman

On patrol, an officer always expects a variety of kid calls. This particular call wasn't mine, though I was involved.

Responding to a call to Twelfth and Birch, the officer on duty found my neighbor, Mrs. Molter sitting on my front porch. She rushed to the squad car.

"Where's Alex? Why didn't they send Alex?"

"Officer O'Kash is off duty for the day. Can I help you?"

"Oh dear. "You've got to find Alex and Annabelle right away."

"What's wrong?"

She preceded to explain what took place earlier in the day.

Her five year old son and four of his friends were playing in her house and watching television. After their favorite program, Superman, her son went into the bathroom and returned with a large bottle of pills.

"These are Superman pills," he told his buddies. "If we take them we'll be able to fly."

The boys ingested several pills each.

When their actions were discovered, Mrs. Molter panicked. The capsules they had taken were her reducing pills - amphetamines. She called her doctor immediately and was told the boys must all have their stomachs pumped.

With plans to hustle the boys to their homes and inform their mothers of the situation, Mrs. Molter had found Danny missing. When she inquired of the other boys, they told her

Danny's mother had called him home and they saw him get into the car with her and drive away.

Mrs. Molter called the hospital to see if, somehow, my wife had learned of the situation and rushed Danny off for treatment.

In the meantime, I had arrived home from duty and as previously planned, my wife was ready and waiting, with Danny, to join me on some errands.

While I carried out my errands at various business and locations throughout town, my wife waited in the car with Danny. Each time I would come back to the car, she complained of how wild the boy was.

"He's wound up like a tin soldier. He won't stop moving. He keeps crawling over the backrest into the front seat and then back again to the rear seat. When he's not crawling he's bouncing - and his mouth hasn't stopped for one second."

I reprimanded my son and continued on my errands, never knowing that several of my fellow officers were always a few calls behind me, unable to catch up.

When we returned home, Mrs. Molter was still sitting on our steps.

"Annabelle, where have you been?"

There wasn't time for my wife to reply before the officer who'd taken Mrs. ? call pulled up behind us. "Alex, we've been trying to catch up with you for more than an hour."

"What's going on here?" I asked.

Mrs. Molter explained. "You've got to get Danny to a hospital right away and get his stomach pumped. The boys got into my reducing pills."

"Oh my God. No wonder he's been acting this way."

Though my wife and I were both concerned, we knew the drill. At five years of age, this would be the fifth time Danny would have his stomach pumped. "Everything goes into his mouth," my wife often lamented.

At the hospital, laying on the table in the emergency room, Dan watched as the nurse applied lubricant to the end of the nasal gastric tube.

"Why are you putting that gunk on that hose?" he asked.

"So it will slide through your nose, down your throat and into your stomach.," the nurse answered him.

Dan, an old had at the procedure, was not only calm but continued to ask questions throughout the procedure.

"What's that gurgling noise?"

"We're pumping out your stomach to get any pills that may be left out of there," he was told.

"If you don't get those pill out, will my skin fall off and will I be a skeleton?"

"Well, I don't think you have to worry about that, we'll get all those pills out, but I don't want to see you back here again young man."

My fellow officer had taken us to the hospital in the squad car making use of the siren lights to get us there as quickly as possible. He told Danny, "There are no pills that will make you fly. When you grow up, you can be an aviator. Then you can fly any time you want."

"What's an aviator?" Danny asked.

~

Pigeon Town USA

Lower Banks Avenue in Superior was also known as Pigeon Town. Two large grain elevators, the Globe and the Great Northern, were located at the foot of Banks Avenue adjacent to the waterfront. Train loads of grain arrived daily to be shipped to the mills on the East Coast. The switching and bumping of cars spilled wheat and other grains along the tracks. Large flocks of pigeons feasted on the fallen seeds. Their appetites satisfied, they would fly to the high buildings in the downtown area to perch and bask in the sun.

Walking down the street, one could hear the coo-cooings as the pigeons strutted back and forth on the rooftops. Walkers who looked up to admire the beautiful plumage of the birds were often greeted with a plunk-plunk, and a splat of bird droppings. As the flocks increased and the condition worsened, pedestrians began to complain. City hall phones were swamped with calls.

Chemicals and other deterrents were used but to no avail. A group of civic minded citizens volunteered to combat the problem. I was the police officer assigned as liaison to the project. Saturday morning armed with 22 rifles, the unit marched down the street in military fashion shooting at the pigeons on the rooftops. The local newspaper published an article praising the efforts of the city fathers contributing to the betterment of the community. The following day, bird lovers flooded the mayor's phone line with complaints and a stop order for pigeon extermination action was issued.

Not long after this series of events, my telephone rang at 3 am, awaking me from a sound sleep.

"This is police headquarters calling. We have another pigeon problem, O'Kash. You'd better come down here right away."

Arriving at the station I was informed my fifteen-year-old son, Tim, and his buddy, Smitty, were apprehended on the roof of the Superior Hotel.

"What in the hell were you doing out at 3 a.m. and why were you up on that roof?" I asked.

"We went there to see if they shot Seymore and Frebba."

"Who the hell are Seymore and Frebba?"

"Our pigeons."

The story unfolded that the boys had taken baby squabs, built pens for them and raised the pigeons.

Tim protested vehemently to the suggestion that he would have to release the pigeons and stay off the roof top of the Superior Hotel. In the end, we reached a compromise. Seymour and Frebba were moved to the roof of our garage, and the family gained first-hand knowledge of contending with the coo-cooing, plunk-plunking and occasional well aimed splat during back-yard barbecues.

Second Hand Smoke

Had I continued my employment with the police force, I probably would have had to file for a disability retirement for secondary smoke inhalation.

As a patrolman I was scheduled to work with different partners. The luck of the draw invariably paired me with a cigar smoking partner. Neither I nor my wife ever smoked and being a non smoker made it difficult to have to constantly inhale second hand smoke for an eight hour shift.

As I mentioned earlier, my wife complained heartily when I returned from work, "smelling like a smoke-house."

Mac loved his cigars and smoked consistently. I tried to appease my wife by saying I would only be working with Mac for two weeks and then I would change partners. Unfortunately, the next two weeks, I would draw another cigar smoker.

Ben smoked cigars, lighting one from another, with little regard to the discomfort it caused others. Further problems existed because Ben wanted the car windows closed due to the cold weather. "I don't like drafts," he always said.

This resulted in eight hours in a closed squad car with no fresh air. My eyes would water, and my throat would become sore and hoarse. My only relief was when we began door checks.

I purposely lagged in checking the doors and windows of the buildings on our beat, staying out of the vehicle as much as possible. It was useless to complain as there were no rules

Alex O'Kash

against smoking on the job. The most I could do was look forward to spring weather, when I was allowed to crack open the window.

Whenever the opportunity came to walk a beat, I gladly volunteered. No matter how cold the weather, I was happy to be able to breath fresh air.

All Good Things

In 1967 there were three police officers performing the duties of Desk Sergeant, Jim Suzens, Carl Renos and myself.

Jim Suzens was interested in a county position that was being vacated - Douglas County Probation and Parole Agent. In order to eligible for the position, one had to take a State Civil Service exam. Jim took the exam, placed high in the scoring and secured the job. After a time, Jim was offered a promotion and relocation to Madison and was considering the position. He suggested that Carl Renos and I take the Civil Service exam and apply for the job he would be vacating.

Carl and I both passed the exam. This resulted in our names being added to a state-wide bank that was drawn on whenever positions opened up. I was contacted several times, once being offered the position of Right-Of-Way Purchasing Agent that would have required relocation to the southern part of the state, and another time for the position of Probation and Parole Agent in Ashland County. Not wanting to relocate my family, I declined the positions offered, stating that I would wait until Jim Suzen's position became available and then apply for that.

Then an opening became available with the Industrial Commission of Wisconsin, at the Job Service office in Superior. My fellow police officer, Renos, was offered the job and turned it down. I was contacted.

I agreed to an interview and a board of three came up from Madison to conduct the two day session.

The position in question involved working with local business owners and managers to encourage them to use the employment office for listing their job openings, and also working with veterans returning to the work force.

Two of the interview board recommended me for the job, but the third dissented, stating that he thought I wasn't qualified. When I pointed out my veteran status, and the fact that I was the post commander of the local VFW chapter, he changed his mind. The job was mine - if I wanted it.

I was concerned about two things. City employees had a very good pension plan. I didn't want to give that up. Also, I was concerned about whether or not I would like the job with the employment service as much as I did police work. The biggest advantage of taking the new position would be the end of shift work. My hours would be 8:30 to 4:30 Monday through Friday. My wife and children were all for that.

An inquiry revealed that city and state employees were all covered under the same pension plan, so I would continue to accrue benefits. As to perhaps not liking the new *white collar* job, I requested a six month leave of absence from the police department, with the option to return if I chose. Granting a leave of absence was highly unusual, but the mayor of Superior at that time was a friend of mine and I was granted the leave.

A return to the department was not in the cards though. I spent thirteen years with the Wisconsin State Employment Service, having been promoted to District Director, covering five offices in Northwest Wisconsin.

Taking that civil service exam, almost on a whim, marked the end of my career as a Superior Police Officer. However, it wasn't quite the end of the story.

Village Cop

Following retirement, I didn't anticipate that I would ever again be involved in police work. Not long after that retirement, however, it was suggested that I run for the office of President of the Village of Lake Nebagamon. I ran, and I won the election. Shortly thereafter I was confronted with the problem of a two month medical leave for the village constable.

Within days of the constable's scheduled hospitalization for knee surgery, I began to receive calls from the villagers. I responded to the complaints and made an attempt to resolve all issues satisfactorily.

At the next board meeting I proposed that we appoint a temporary Marshall to serve in the absence of the constable. My request was denied. I was told arrangements had been made with Douglas County Sheriff's Department to handle all serious crimes in the absence of the constable.

Calls continued at my residence. Explanations to the callers that we had no acting police official in Lake Neb␣␣mon and they would have to call the sheriff's departme␣ ␣ot appease the callers.

"I am a taxpayer and I demand that so␣ immediately," I heard more than once.

I received all nature of calls, one f␣ to report a couple fornicating on the v␣␣ across from his home, another, a w␣

the abundance of algae in the lake was due to someone dumping chemical pollutants in the water.

I tried my best to pacify those who called me by providing what services I could to resolve their problems. Needless to say I was relieved and pleased with the return of the constable and the end of complaint calls to my house.

At the next board meeting I submitted a gas expense of $12.00 for the use of my vehicle for 300 miles of travel for calls and patrol duty for the two months of the village constable's absence. The expense was denied.

I guess in public service you're damned if you do and damned if you don't.

A Policeman's Work Is Never Done

As I'm putting the final touches on these stories of my years in law enforcement, I am approaching my 74th birthday. Thankfully I am still in relatively good health, having recovered from by-pass surgery performed a year ago. I am enjoying my retirement, my lake home and these quiet days with my wife, and my youngest daughter and her family, also living in Lake Nebagamon. I look forward to visits from my other children and grandchildren. Usually, one of those visits coincides with the annual Lake Nebagamon Summerfest.

One of the attractions during the village festival is a fine arts exhibit. Many valuable pieces of artwork are displayed in the grade school gymnasium. In recent years, after an incident involving vandalism and damage to some of the artwork, guards have been hired to stay overnight in the gymnasium during Summerfest.

My daughter is involved in much of the volunteer work coordinated by the Lake Nebagamon Community Association, who in turn sponsors and organizes the Summerfest activities. Returning from the most recent meeting of the Community Association, she had a little surprise for me.

"Say Dad . . . Kay asked if you could do us a little favor."

Knowing that my daughter always looks out for my welfare, I assumed the favor was one she thought I could handle. "Sure," I said. "What is it?"

"The gymnasium will be open for several hours Friday morning so that the artists can bring in their work for display," she explained. "They haven't been able to hire a guard for those hours - "

She hesitated purposely and from the grin that spread across her face I knew what was coming.

"Do you suppose you could keep an eye on the place - make sure the riff-raff stays out?"

"Is this legitimate, or are you just looking for another chapter in the book?"

"Honest, Dad, I didn't suggest this. Kay came up with it all on her own."

"But - ?" I asked, knowing there was more.

"But you have to admit, it makes a great ending."

And so it does.

A Police Officer's Prayer

Lord, I ask for courage -
Courage to face and
conquer my own fears . . .
Courage to take me
where others will not go . . .

I ask for strength -
Strength of body to protect others,
and strength of spirit
to lead others . . .

I ask for dedication -
Dedication to my job, to do it well,
Dedication to my community,
to keep it safe . . .

Give me, Lord, concern
for those who trust me,
and compassion for those
who need me . . .

And please, Lord,
through it all,
be at my side.

To order additional copies of
Stop In The Name Of The Law
send $9.95 check or money order to -
Savage Press
P.O. Box 115
Superior, WI 54880

or

to charge your order to your M.C. or Visa account,
call

1-800-732-3867

Savage Press publishes **The Northern Reader**
magazine, novels, short stories, poetry, family histories,
memoirs, post cards, Christmas cards and promotional
material of all kinds. We are firmly rooted the good soil
of creative words. We believe there is health and
personal growth available to all who submit to the
writing process. We want to be a viable voice for all
who seek enrichment through creative writing. Please
feel free to submit your typed, double spaced work for
consideration. If you would like more information on
how to get your book or other material published,
contact Savage Press at Box 115, Superior, WI 54880,
or call (715) 394-9513 with your questions.